THE
MARKETING
CHECKLIST 2

THE

MARKETING

CHECKLIST 2

49 More Simple Ways to Master Your Marketing

Hank Yuloff

Naked Book Publishing

This is for my partner and my brain, Sharyn Yuloff.
She works her tail off on every part of our life
and I am more than appreciative for everything she does.

I love you, baby!!!
You're the best!

Contents

For access to other resources, videos, and information go to:
www.SedonaMarketingRetreats.com/TMC2

(This is our way of teaching you how to use inside pages on your website to market yourself. See? We've started sharing things already!)

The Scary Part of Change
Is the Best Part of Change

"Your life does not get better by chance, it gets better by change."
Jim Rohn

*"The secret of change is to focus all of your energy, not on fighting the old,
but on building the new."*
Socrates

"I am always ready to learn although I do not like being taught."
Winston Churchill

*"Incremental changes come from technology.
Breakthrough change comes from people."*
Jesper Lowgren

*"I may not always be looking for game change,
but I am always looking for a change reaction.*
Hank Yuloff

Looking as far back as childhood, I was not always an early adopter of change—in fact, at times I feared it, but as we built our business and had major changes in where we lived, I use memories of past changes to stay focused. I know this: To continue our success, change is necessary.

As I was writing this book, we were making one of those immense and all-encompassing changes in our business and our personal lives. I began to recall other times when change had been necessary.

When I became the sales manager for my college newspaper, *The Daily Aztec* at San Diego State preceding my senior year, I spent every day of the summer getting ready for the coming school year. Prior to our sales people showing up, there were trainings to plan, collection matters from the previous year, customer lists to create, special editions to get ready to sell, and more. I prepared and I over-prepared. This attention to preparation resulted in the highest sales of any year in the history of the newspaper.

As the sales manager for a promotional products company that I worked for before opened Promotionally Minded, I had to continuously change the way we train to adjust to the marketplace. My monthly newsletter and yearly training book are how my team share what is working at the moment to increase our sales.

When it comes to our radio show, we have gone from hours of preshow prep to ninety minutes to thirty minutes. We have learned how to be well prepared enough that our show is smooth and efficient.

When I look at the evolution of our business over a period of seven years, I can see competitors who are still selling promotional products using decades old models, I see a vast difference between us and them, and an equally vast difference in the way in which we are able to serve our clients and in our ability to attract forward-thinking clients.

Each time I look at a new venture, and feel a fear of change, I get over it by starting to make checklists—not only in my head but by writing them down. There are checklists on how to market the business, and on operational details. And there are checklists for planning our customer experience: what we need to do before our clients show up, what we will teach them, and what will be needed to coach them afterwards.

What I have learned from experience is that being prepared—over-prepared—is my key to being the most accepting of change and to using it to an advantage

I have faith in myself, faith in relationship, faith that I am better at change than I think I am. After all, what's the worst thing that could happen—I could get stuck? Well, there's a checklist to get over those things, too. Let's get started.

1

Name It or Rename It

I am asked all the time, "How do I get started with a marketing plan?" We're going to answer that question in this book.

My last book, *The Marketing Checklist . . . 80 Simple Ways to Master Your Marketing*, laid the groundwork. By identifying different tactics, best practices, tips, and strategies, it was more than 150 pages on ways to market your company. After I put that book to bed, I realized that there were many things I still wanted to say—especially about marketing plans.

So, getting back to that marketing plan question, the short answer is (and you are going to get this a lot from me)—it depends. I think there are a few things which are tied for first. Some of them may not apply to your business, depending on the age of your business and the success you are enjoying.

The first thing you are going to have to do is name it. What is the name of your company?

Okay, all you I-don't-need-this-section people, not so fast!

If you are an established business, you may come up with a different, proprietary product or system for doing what you do. In our company's case it was the OurMarketingGuy.com system for creating marketing plans for our clients. This market planning division of our company was different, though it worked in sync with the promotional product wing of our corporation. We had clients which bought from both divisions, but most of our clients bought from one or the other, and we wanted each one to stand out. When we began our marketing boot camps in Sedona, Arizona, that business needed its own name, too—Sedona Marketing Retreats.

You can see that the Sedona company had a location, and what we did in the name was similar to what we did when we created OurMarketingGuy. The idea was for people to say, "You need marketing? You need to call our marketing guy. He takes care of all our needs." Promotionally Minded, the promotional products company, remained as the overall corporate name, but it had been used strictly for promotional products for more than fifteen years prior to our adding the market planning wing and we felt it had been established for just that service.

We had a client that did mold testing for real estate agents. Since it was considered to be a conflict of interest for them to do the repair work too, he set up a different company with a different name to do that work. He operated them separately and was very upfront about the ties between the two companies, but when he wanted to promote one service, or the other, it made sense for that firewall to exist, hence the different names.

Many companies have names which have evolved. For example, Philip Morris became Altria Group (and they still would not sell me PM.com). Blackwater USA, best known for being killers for hire, became XE Services then Academi after some of its employees killed the wrong people. Arthur Anderson got embroiled with Enron and had to change its name to Accenture. You get the point.

I don't want you to think that something *bad* has to happen. We have begun to evolve our company name to Sedona Marketing from the original Promotionally Minded. New city, enlarged focus, new name.

And one more very famous example: Back in 1893, a North Carolina pharmacist named Caleb Bradham started experimenting with a few soft drink recipes. One of these bore his name—Brad's Drink. In 1898 Brad's Drink was renamed to Pepsi Cola and would become one of the world's most recognized brands.

The most famous example of using different names for different parts of a company is General Motors, which created Chevrolet, Pontiac, Oldsmobile, Buick, Cadillac, and later Saturn as different portions of their corporation to produce different, albeit similar automobiles.

So what to name your business? Here are a few tips:

- Using the geographic term for where you operate is far from sexy or unique but it does help your target market find you. In Sedona, there are dozens of company names which begin with the words Red Rock or Sedona. Using an area helps in search engine optimization, too. (We bought the URL SFVAcupuncture.com for a client because people in the San Fernando Valley quite often use *SFV* as the search term.
- That URL story leads me to address the issue of checking to see if your URL is available. You may have the coolest name for a company, but if it has already been purchased, you are out of luck. Prior to buying OurMarketingGuy.com, it was going to have a similar name, but that similar name had already been taken. As it turns out, I got lucky because I was able to use an *OMG* in my new company's logo. That was far superior to what it was going to be originally. That

only happened because I checked the URL availability prior to filling out any paperwork for registering the name.

- In addition to the URL, check all the social media. At the time of this writing, there is a website called NameChk.com which allows you to check dozens at one time.
- Cute is okay, but make sure that it has lasting value. We once saw a restaurant named Frying Nemo, which was wonderful when the movie *Finding Nemo* had just come out, but going down the road ten years it seems dated. When I went to college in San Diego there was a chain of restaurants called Godfather Pizza. They used the same typeface that was used in the movie. Or there was Indiana Bones—Temple of Groom (do-it-yourself dog-washing store).
- Don't be afraid to change your name. Many companies have done that to give their clients a new, fresh view of their company.
- Watch out for sexual innuendo and double entendre. For example, do not name your pet-grooming place "Doggie Styles," or your chimney-sweep business "Ash Wipe," or your window repair place "Pane in the Glass."

We are A-okay when it comes to the name of our business.
◯ YES   ◯ NO

We might want to give one of our products or services their own brand name.
◯ YES   ◯ NO

2

The Difference between Branding, Advertising, Public Relations, and Marketing

Business owners are constantly bombarded by four terms that seem to get used interchangeably as if they all mean the same thing. In order to get what you need from a consultant that you are thinking of hiring, here are some easy-to-understand definitions. What's most important to remember is that this is the communications function of your company.

Advertising
This is the easiest of these four sisters to understand. It is the only one of them over which you have complete control. Advertisements are paid messages placed in any media (print, direct mail, television, radio, billboards, digital, promotional products, anything that can carry your message), which is then placed in front of the eyeballs of your target market. This is the least believable part of your communications so it has to be transparently educational along with being the sizzle that promotes your company.

Branding
This is the image of your company. It's the message you wish to present. It's what you want people to think about when they think of your company. This is your brand.

It includes your logo, and the colors you use. It's your slogan, and the thing that stays in their mind when your message is no longer in front of them.

Your brand is your company's personality. This is why I always tell solo-preneurs that *they* are the brand of their company.

Public Relations
There are many different groups (or stakeholders) that are important to your business. They are employees, vendors, customers of various kinds, your board of directors, the press, and anyone else who effects your bottom line. Public relations is the practice of creating the messages you wish each of those groups to hear and the dissemination of those messages to them. The maintenance

of these relationships can be vital. Think of them as much needed third-party validations when the press or a blog or a website mentions your company.

When you read that a company has a *public-relations nightmare* you are either hearing that a company has not prepared for this type of event or that the writer is putting their own imprint on the story. Either way, it is good to have a list of potential challenges, and prepared statements of things you would want to say to each of your groups. It can reside in a three-ring binder on the shelf, but it should exist in print and digital form. It is important that you choose the one person who is to be on-camera or on-microphone as a spokesperson in all matters that deal with your company in advance of any issue. This can become a problem for non-profits; it's not uncommon that any board member feels they have the authority to speak for the organization.

Marketing
This is the overall umbrella under which all the others function, plus we add the sales department. Marketing is the overall act of promoting or selling your product. It includes market research, where you decide to place your building, and all of your collateral materials (like your website, social media pages, and brochures). It encompasses your product packaging, and how you package your services and events.

We have looked at having a public-relations stand-by plan.
◯ YES   ◯ NO

We have a firm handle on the performance of each of these functions.
◯ YES   ◯ NO

We could use assistance here.
◯ YES   ◯ NO

3

How Much Is That Doggy in the Window?

The question of pricing will always come up with clients—sometimes it's the only thing on their mind. The answer to, "How much do you charge?" goes hand in hand with you asking them, "How much are you willing to pay?" If business owners knew the answer to the second question, the first question would become irrelevant.

Let's pretend we do know the answer and like most marketing goals: Begin with the end in mind and work towards that outcome.

Here is what I mean.

In late 2015, Disneyland announced that for the first time in its sixty-year history, it was going to begin offering targeted pricing. Their goal was to even out the attendance in their parks, and provide them with overall higher profits. By charging more during the period when most people wanted to be there (holiday break between Christmas and New Year), would result in not having to turn people away when they reached capacity, because *just enough* people would be dissuaded from coming at the busiest days (when they would be full anyway and already making close to maximum profit). It would fill more of the park on days with lower pricing when people were less likely to arrive at the Happiest Place on Earth, which would be a Tuesday through Thursday in September or October when children were in school and not as likely to be able to attend with their parents. For economic reasons, there *will* be enough parents who will pull their kids from school for a less expensive day visiting The Mouse to make it worth it. Add that to the people who do not have children and have more flexibility in their schedules and who do not want to share the park with two thousand baby strollers.

Price is measuring people's resistance to change. What are the rules here about price?

- If it is too high, they won't pay it.
- If it is close to what they want, you are up against the this-or-that theory and competing against something else they would rather get ("Would we rather go to Disneyland on a Wednesday in October, or spend a weekend in Las Vegas?").
- If it is too low, the clients will wonder (they won't always ask) if it they will get their value's worth. When I began producing marketing

plans, we charged an amount that was so low that people did not think they were going to get anything worthwhile.
- Are your costs covered and will you make enough to turn a profit?

Let's use the "It's Time for a Haircut" story.

I could go to the local barber shop and get a men's haircut for about $15. I could go to Supercuts and get a trim for about $25 including a tip. I could go to a private hair dresser who rents a chair at a salon for about $50. I could go to the owner of that shop and get charged about $100.

I have done all of these but tend to end up at the local chain hair-cutting place for a few reasons: price, no need to set an appointment, convenient to my place of work. Why am I not going to the two higher-priced options? Because, like most men, I do not see the difference in my haircut. And I do not put any value in the social aspect of heading to a salon. And I am just getting the cut, not all of the other things that can be done to the follicles on my head. I have done the salon thing, and have enjoyed the few times that I have done it, but not one of the several women who have cut my hair have made the experience worth the extra cost.

People will pay for the highest *perceived* value. They will pay for the outcome. If the price is too low, they will say that "she does not know what she is doing." If the price is too high, their "no thank you" is quite often the feedback you will need to adjust your pricing for the next time.

Here is another way to look at it. Answer the question, "What problem, or struggle, or desire do you solve?" For each one of these, there is a promise or a pay-off which will result in a sale. Talk to people about what their struggles are, add your genius, and then you can charge for it. The perception on their end that you can deliver, and the confidence on your end that you can solve their problem is what will determine what your price is going to be.

In Sedona, our Sedona Marketing Retreats boot camps have been successful because we found the price that worked. We grouped demographically similar business owners together (women-owned, LGBT, medical, legal, financial, etc.). We gave them solid solutions to the specific challenges that they faced. We got rid of their feeling of overwhelm as it related to marketing their product or service. We gave them their marketing plan. We then followed up with them in group calls for a period of time after their long weekend in our retreat center. Oh, and we had them participate in fun, social activities that the area lends itself to. That last item is one of the features that makes us unique.

In *The Marketing Checklist*, we talk about a unique selling proposition—USP. When we price, we put it into action.

Our USP at Sedona Marketing Retreats: "I teach business owners what to say about their company and more importantly how to say it so that they are wildly successful. We do all this using the power of Sedona to energize their sales and marketing efforts."

Take a moment here to figure out your unique selling proposition. Ask these questions, then answer them:

- What will make people realize how good I am?
- What will make people pay me what I am worth? (Because I am the best at what I do.)

_____

_____

_____

_____

_____

_____

We have a firm grasp of what our clients will pay for our services.
○ YES   ○ NO

4

Ladies and Gentlemen, Now Presenting . . .

One of the best ways to present your product is through group presentations. We put a group of prospects, sales people, and sometimes current clients together, and talk about why we have a great product. Here are seven tips on making your presentations successful.

1. If there are five salespeople bringing people together for a presentation, the best presenter is at the front of the room. Period. When you have live prospects who are taking a look at your product, it is not the time for someone to practice their presentation skills.

   Let's say you are a financial planning firm and you have put together a "Lunch and Learn" at your office. Are you going to let the guy who barely knows how figure out how to value a company present your list of the twenty up and coming investment targets? And if that person *does* know how to describe the process, if they do not know how to make eye contact, think on their feet, or know how to speak from their diaphragm to the farthest part of the room, why put him or her up there? Use your best speaker and let the rest of the team be in the room, laughing at the appropriate times, smiling and nodding their heads in agreement, and being completely supportive. When the guy who wants to be at the front of the room, but can only stare at his feet takes twenty-five Toastmaster classes, then you can think about putting him up in front.

2. Start and end on time. I am one of the easiest people in the world to sell to. I love to buy. But in a group presentation, if you start late and therefore end late, I am a no-sale person. Why disrespect the people who did show up and are ready to learn at the appointed time.

3. Remember—no one is signing up or buying while the speaker is speaking, so if you told people to take an hour out of their life to check something out, set your presentation time for thirty-five minutes and leave twenty minutes for questions. Your potential client will love you even more if you save them some time by finishing early.

4. Since there *will* be late comers, know they are a distraction. Leave a few seats in the back for them. You can even tell everyone that those seats are for the tardy people. It makes them feel special that you have their comfort in mind.

5. Involve several people in the event. Have official greeters so that the speaker is not meeting people at the door. She is the star, so don't have her take tickets and pass out the popcorn.

6. People want to do two things: Make money and have fun. Having fun needs to come first so have music playing when they arrive, use gifts as an incentive for showing up, raffles, funny stories and for heaven's sake, don't forget to smile!

7. Have several different presentations prepared so that when you are asked to speak at someone else's event, you can give them a list of topics from which to choose. Here is my topic list:
   10 Ways to Market Your Business without Leaving Your Office
   23 (Mostly) Inexpensive Ways to Market Your Business
   The Marketing Checklist
   10 Ways Promotional Product Distributors Fail at Self Promotion
   20 Ways You Can Have Fun While Promoting Your Business

We have 3 different programs to present to an audience.
◯ YES ◯ NO

If no, we will create them.
◯ YES ◯ NO

5

Create an Official Referral Program

We created a referral program for a dentist that was to attract new business. We wanted to get her clients involved in building her practice since in the professional world, happy clients are the best source of new business.

We created a point system for her to market her business, and we formalized a rewards program for her clients to send her referrals. Here are some of the ideas we used so that she could give away points. This is just a beginning.

- 2 points whenever a patient sends an email to a friend. They can earn up to 200 points per month via this program. That email should say: "Hi there! I just wanted to say hello and introduce you to a friend of our family. Her name is Jane Dentist and she is our family's dentist. We would love for you to make an appointment and go see Dr. Dentist. If you do, we will both get a $10 gift card to _____ coffee shop."
- 3 points whenever a patient helps with sending a out a card. The patient provides the name and address and a picture is taken with Dr. Dentist. The card will say, "You were referred to us by (patient's name)," and will then offer specials. They can earn a maximum of 60 points per month.
- 50 points for a 5-star review on _____ website.
- 100 points when they walk through the door for their appointment.
- 100 points when one of their friends set an appointment.
- 100 more points when that friend walks in the door.
- 200 more points the second time a family member walks through the door for an appointment.
- 300 points for filming a video testimonial for the practice.

The number of points can be varied and we use points because they have no specific value.

The next part of this program is the rewards part. We came up with ten different ways for the patients to redeem the points with our client. What you create, depends on the budget you have for this program. We have clients who use promotional products (t-shirts, computer bags, or pens) to gift cards or discounts on services.

If you go the discount route, try giving those discounts on products that your clients are not already buying from you, so you expand your sales while giving them the gift of you.

We have a referral program
○ YES ○ NO

No, but we should create one.
○ YES ○ NO

6

Your Future Profits Can Be Based on Five Things

I once attended a sales presentation and heard a theory that was put forward by Harvard business professor Michael E. Porter. I think it makes a lot of sense for us to evaluate our businesses using this particular tool. This model identifies and analyzes five competitive forces that shape every industry, and helps determine an industry's weaknesses and strengths. I'm going to use my company as an example of how to work through the model and show how it effects portions of my business. How do you think it effects yours?

1. **Competition in the industry. Is there a lot?** From the promotional product part of our company, yes, there is! I think I am different from most of my competitors in that I think it is healthy for our industry if many of them are doing well. If they fail, that means that there are fewer companies sending orders to companies I use to manufacture the products (mugs, pens, calendars, clothing with logos), which gives me a less stable supply chain.

2. **Potential of new entrants into industry.** There is a medium high bar to enter our industry. You have to be creative, and be able to grasp how most of the products are used to target business. Well over 80% of people in their first year of sales in our industry disappear within the first year.

3. **Power of suppliers.** How much power does one supplier have over you? This item effects companies that sell products far more than companies that offer a service. For our company, the factories which make the products we sell are very important. Luckily for us, there are very few monopolies.

4. **Power of customers.** If you have few clients, and lose one, a much higher percentage of your business disappears. If you have a thousand roughly equal clients, then losing one makes less of a difference.

15

5. Threat of substitute products. Are there other services or products that are similar to yours? Can your place can be taken? Ouch. All of us have to think about this. On the marketing side of our company, there is less threat because of what we do, and where and how we do it.

Our customer base is large enough.
○ YES   ○ NO

7

Preparing to Be Interviewed

One of your goals to market your business should be to get interviewed—as often as possible. Interviews published in print, on the internet, or in video or audio form are incredible third-party validation for your company.

We want to be prepared for them, however, because doing things "off the cuff" is not the best way to tell your story; it often does not come off the way you want it to be told.

Here are some tips for being prepared:

1. You need headshot business photos of various kinds. Using cell phone pictures may be okay for posting on social media, but *not* as your official business shot. It is not expensive and you will be seen in a much more professional light when you hire a photographer.

2. You should create four or five biographies, of various lengths for the different places you will need them. One will be a couple of sentences for a photo caption, all the way up to various longer ones, which will be used in interviews and your book.

3. Interviewers will want to ask you questions, so why not give them the questions that you want them to ask you. This way you can create the narrative, rather than use theirs. If you want to help them do their job, add the answers to those questions. This is especially helpful for radio interviews because they have a limited amount of time to fill between commercial breaks and they can gauge which questions will work the best on their particular show. Believe it or not they appreciate this!

4. You need video clips as well. Lots of them. Why not answer some of the questions from the list above.

5. Another type of video you need is B-roll. This is video of you going about doing what you do. When they interview you, they do not

need to have a camera on you all the time, they can show the B-Roll while you speak. For example, let's say they were interviewing Larry Broughton, who owns Broughton Hotels. They may ask him about one of his boutique properties and show B-Roll video of the hotel while they use his verbal description. Four or five thirty-second clips should do it, but add as many as you want.

6. You will need a place for all of this information to reside, which should be as a private page of your website. By private, I mean, if someone does not know how to get there, they cannot stumble upon it when they go through your site. Although there is an About Us page button on my website, which takes people to a page that has my story, there is no Biography page button. But when you go to www. OurMarketingGuy.com/bio you will see that I have many things reporters will be able to use. There are several types of photos, a few biographies of various lengths, and many questions and answers that they will be able to use. We have also added video B-roll, which will be used by reporters.

7. *Read* what the interviewer has done recently and mention it to them.

8. Remember to keep adding more photos and videos to this page. Keep it fresh and grow the material.

9. As you are interviewed, add the logos of the various outlets who have interviewed you to the page. You can also add links to those interviews.

**I am ready if my local TV station calls
and asks to interview me today at 5 p.m.**
○ YES   ○ NO

8

Is the Chicken and the Egg Marketing Working for You?

What? You say that the question is "what came first the chicken *or* the egg?" Not in marketing. In marketing it is the chicken *and* the egg. You have to be telling your story all the time, not waiting to have your chicken grow up and laying eggs, or have the perfect egg to produce the perfect chicken.

One morning at a chamber of commerce breakfast, Johan Montoya of BoostHealthNow.com and I were talking about how he could increase his sales. Johan had just stood up at the breakfast and told people that if they wanted more information on his biology-based restorative health agency, they should *not* go to his website, but go to him directly. He wants to help them with bio guidance, the theory that to develop a health balance, the human body needs to eat properly, breathe, sleep, and eliminate waste. And that "everything else is a sales pitch."

From our discussion, Johan said that people were not going to his website anyway, so why send them there. "Besides," he said, "our company is evolving and that website does not tell our story the way we want to tell it." And it was going to take money, which they did not currently have (lots, evidently, because it was not built in WordPress, but rather on one of those replicated site platforms that do not help your SEO at all).

The method of marketing your services is constantly evolving. Today, if you rely on people being sold only on your face-to-face meetings, you are eliminating an entire world of possibilities. Those people are also going to check your site out anyway, just to make sure they made the right decision. It's the chicken and the egg marketing. Neither of the two came first, they work together.

With the chicken and the egg marketing, you have to tell your story, knowing that it is not complete. By example, if you were reading this chapter as a blog post on the OurMarketingGuy.com site, it would be just one blog. Helpful, but just one piece of the Our Marketing Guy story. This post, however, when seen together with lots of other posts, which were written over time—the development of the chicken from the egg to adulthood—will help you decide to hire my company to assist you with marketing *your* company.

And let's pull the curtain back for a moment. After this blog is finished, tagged, and promoted, I am going to share it with Johan and have him notice that in pretty quick order, since I mentioned him and told a bit of his incredible story, my post may rank among the highest searches for his name and his company name. His ranking will change when he does a few things:

1. Rebuild his site in WordPress.

2. Blog more.

3. Answer the ten questions (one per blog post) that people ask him all the time, so he can send people to his website for information. This also helps build that bond between you and your potential clients.

4. Answer the ten questions (again, one per blog post) that Johan wishes people would ask him.

5. More video. Lots more. Tons more. Just like this blog (yes, it was originally a blog post) was introduced with a video (also tagged and key-word coded to both my company and Johan's), his posts can be, too. Let's let our potential clients gather information they way they want to. It could be by video, or the written word.

My chicken and egg marketing is working.
○ YES   ○ NO

How could it be improved?

_____

_____

_____

_____

_____

9

How He Talked Himself Out of the Sale

The concept of "How Salespeople Talk Themselves Out of the Sale" has been rolling around in my head for a long time and at a networking meeting this morning, there it was again. A salesman managed to completely close the gate on the road to the sale—with *me*!

In the middle of the pre-meeting throng, I saw a financial planner that I was friendly with (occupation changed to protect the ignorant), so I said hello. He asked me how my wife was (sometimes she shows up at these meetings) and then said, "You know, can we step over here for a moment?"

When we were off to the side, he said, "Did you know that you never ask me how I am doing?"

"What?"

"You don't ask me how I am doing. It's as if you have zero interest in me."

Those who know me know would say that I am rarely at a loss for words, and since I thought I was always rather engaged with this person, I could not understand why this salesperson was reprimanding me this way.

Taken completely off guard, I apologized to him for his impression, said that certainly was not intent, and that I'd try and do better.

He replied, "Well, if I noticed it, others probably do, too."

Interestingly, when we sat down to our breakfast, he sat across from me, and instead of listening to the front-of-the-room speakers, and to each person standing to give their elevator speech, he spent most of the time on his phone checking Facebook, or in a private conversation with the woman next to him. Perhaps she was asking him questions.

I've taken a long road to get to the point, but here it is: I am in the process (and it's a long one) of finding a new financial planner and this gentleman was one of the people I have been watching to see if our personalities and his methods and theories of investing matched mine. He was *this* close to closing the sale.

A while ago, I grabbed the URL HowYouLostTheSale.com for stories like this and I can definitely say that when we build out that site off of the OurMarketingGuy.com site this story will appear there.

What possible outcome did he envision by asking me these questions? What change in behavior towards him does he seek? Actually, I am pretty certain I am going to go out of my way to *avoid* him rather than engage.

We want to use the Law of Attraction to make people want to be around us, instead of being repelled by us. This story is an example that reminds us all that we are being watched. He's single, has a three-bedroom home in Woodland Hills that he lives in with his dachshund and no others. He and his wife split up a while ago and she has some medical issues. They have two grown children and he was formerly a home inspector and in the entertainment industry (sound mixing) prior to his current job. Yep— I know nothing about him.

I have seen someone talk themselves into and right out of a sale.
○ YES ○ NO

10

Feeling Pressure to Perform? Give Yourself a Break

Golf, to me, is one of those sports that carries a great pressure to perform. At the professional level, you have fans surrounding you in judgmental silence. Since I am not much of a golfer, when I play, I could choose to feel that pressure to perform, or, I could ignore it and just have fun. There is a correlation between playing that sport and what we do in our daily occupations.

Let's take the example of Tiger Woods. He has had challenges of many types in the last three years, but after the first three rounds of the 2015 Masters Golf Tournament, he was in contention for the win. Then came hole number one. The announcers mentioned that of all the holes Tiger has played at The Masters, the first tee shot was the most difficult.

And I could understand. Talk about pressure to perform! Tiger is still one of the three or four most recognized golfers in the world so can you imagine stepping up to that first shot of the day? On the last day of the tournament, Tiger hooked the shot into the ninth fairway (the hole that is parallel to the first hole fairway), not exactly where you want to be. He is such a good golfer, and had done that *so* many times at Augusta, that he knew how to recover and saved par on that hole.

Following in Tiger's footsteps, twenty-two-year-old Jordan Spieth, in his second Masters tournament, not only ignored pressure to perform but set a record for being the first golfer ever to be nineteen shots under par (average) for the tournament on his way to winning it.

How does that same pressure to perform affect each of us? I would not enjoy having a bunch of amateur targeted-marketing tacticians standing around, with beer in hand, watching me create a demographically perfect marketing plan for a couple who owns a small company together but who rarely get a chance to get away for a few days to recharge and reactivate their sales (small plug there for our upcoming Sedona Marketing Retreats).

I think, though, many of us put too much pressure to perform upon ourselves and when we hit the occasional bogey (that's one over par, a little worse than the expected average) we let it bother us too long. Didn't make that sale? Need more clients or the right kind of clients? Take a step back, breathe, and get back to your plan.

I am great at giving myself a breather.
○ YES ○ NO

If no, I am getting better!
○ YES ○ NO

11

Search Engine Optimization

I had a call from a friend named Lynn who lives in Michigan. She was at a networking meeting talking with one of her clients— a doctor's office, and they had gotten a call from somebody talking about SEO (search engine optimization). They had been looking for someone that could do it for them, and they were asking Lynn's opinion.

She does not do SEO, and so she asked me if we could. When I asked her what kind of marketing they were doing, she said that they said they didn't have time to blog so they just wanted someone to do it for them.

My thought was "isn't that just great." So here's the analogy I'm going to use with them: If I have heart problems and I could just take a pill rather than change my habits, wouldn't everybody prefer that option? My guess is that we'd all rather just take a pill than change our habits. And there is no magic pill that takes care of *all* heart problems.

SEO works the same way. If it was easy to simply change the keywords in the background of your site, and if it was easy to avoid changing your website and still have it be seen by the search engines as relevant and trusted (even though it was completely static), everyone would do it. But we know that not everyone can be on the first page of search engines.

The reality is that non-static sites, the ones that constantly change are considered to be more trusted and more relevant. In other words the search engine is saying, "It's changing, therefore it's more invested in the success and positive growth of the internet."

I am sure you have heard the expression "If it were easy, everyone would be able to do it." Well, in the case of search engine optimization, if it required very little effort, or in terms of the internet, if one did not have to put in any effort at all, to rank number one on Google and Bing and all the search engines, it would make internet marketing a more confusing thing.

Here's the good news and the bad news all wrapped up together: It isn't easy. You're going to have to work at it a bit. You'll have to blog. And change those keywords, preferably the ones at the top of each page of your website where most web designers just name the title of the page (they call the Contact Us page, *Contact Us* instead of using a term like *Contact The Best*

25

Marketing Company In Los Angeles). You're going to have to make your website change all the time.

It's why we're always adding blogs to the OurMarketingGuy.com page. We are not immune to the rules, and that's the simple truth.

It also helps if your website is built in WordPress because that program is more easily scrolled by all the search engines and as it is open code the search engines feel better about promoting it.

If you need some help with SEO, understand that there is a right way of doing it; don't be charged thousands of dollars just to change your keywords.

Our search engine optimization is incredible.
◯ YES ◯ NO

12

"Get on the Front Page of Google for $199" and other Black-Hat SEO Liars

I got a call from one of our marketing-plan clients. He said that he has been bombarded by calls from a company saying they can get him on the front page of Google and other wild promises.

As his marketing department, I called them back, got Mathew on the phone, and asked, "How?"

"Search engine optimization," he said.

"Really? How?"

"Well, key words, and optimizing, and back links and . . . *blah blah blah.*" He used a bunch of terms designed to confuse and obfuscate, but one stuck with me—back links. Huh?

I asked him where those links are coming from.

"That is proprietary . . ." Huh? Back links should be coming from *trusted* websites and for legitimate purposes—they quote your blog, or you theirs, for example.

I pointed out that if he cannot tell me how is going to give back links to my client, he is probably doing some Black Hat SEO stuff, which would hurt my customer. His only response was, "Well, I guess we cannot work together." Wow! He sure knows what the term *Black Hat* means.

Black Hat SEO is when someone does not follow the rules set up by Google, Yahoo, Bing, and other search engines designed to create a level playing field. Black Hat SEO back links would just be putting links to your website in lots of places, such as another website's blog comments, which have nothing to do with their blog content, however your web URL is read by the search engines and gives you credit for being there. It's not cool.

If there is Black Hat SEO, then there must be White Hat SEO, too, right? Yes. I am going to give you an example of White Hat SEO when I tell you to get more information at the blog site of my wife, Sharyn Yuloff. I will create a link that takes you to somewhere else for more relevant information.

Are there White Hat SEO providers? Yes! Those providers can show you a list of lots of clients who are deliriously happy when you call them.

So how *do* you get better search engine optimization?

- Make sure your website's title pages (top left, above where you are reading the URL) are filled with key words instead of *Contact Us, Blog,* or *Services.* When someone searches for "marketing help in Los Angeles"—that is what they are typing into key searches, not "Our-MarketingGuy Contact Us." You would be amazed at how many web developers inadvertently hurt their clients by doing that.
- Make sure your website is mobile friendly so that when people look at your site from their portable devices, it is easy to read (for example, your phone number shows up as a clickable link, instantly dialing your number). This is *very* important.
- Update your website frequently by blogging.
- Register your website with all the large search engines (do a Google search for a list of them . . . wink wink).
- Gather *lots* of social proof in the form of video testimonials.
- For a lot more tips, check outSharyn Yuloff's blog! You can find it at www.ThatSaysItAll.com. (*See what I did?* I just sent a back links to one of Sharyn's inside pages—these are the best to get, and will give you some good information on building your business.

Attention business owners: When you get calls for SEO promising that for $199 a month they can put you on the front page of *anything* . . . they are *lying, lying, lying, lying,* and using Black Hat SEO. Or they are using your money to buy ads, which, of course, are found at the top of each search (*still lying*)!

I will not fall for SEO pretenders.
◯ YES   ◯ NO, we have to correct an issue

13

Generational Communication of Your Marketing Message

During Promotionally Minded Marketing Days, I had a section in the workshop workbook called "Generational Communication of Your Marketing Message." The short version of that is if you are selling to a grandmother and her grand kid, you have to talk to them differently. And use different tools to speak to them.

While I was discussing generational communication, I noticed that in the room I had a seventy-year-old woman, a fifty-nine-year-old mom of two, a forty-four-year-old male personal trainer, and a set of sixteen-year-old twin brothers. I instantly called a classroom audible and asked them to come to the front of the room to talk about how they receive messages.

Jaws dropped when our sixteen-year-old guest said, among other things, that he has never *seen* either a fax machine or a rotary phone. At the other end of the spectrum, our oldest attendee remembered that hand writing letters to friends, family, and companies when you were disappointed with their service was common. For her, 78 RPM albums were the standard. For our fifty-nine-year-old it was 45s, for the trainer, 33s were common, and our sixteen-year-old gets all his music in MP3 format.

This example will explain a lot about generational communication of your marketing message. Remember it when trying to put together your messages.

How you change your message to different target markets depends on what you are selling. If you are trying to sell a product on an impulse, don't ask someone born in the middle of the last century. They want to keep their cash, compared to Gen Yers (born in the last quarter of the century) who are more apt to not save as much.

Are you using music in the background of your ads? Use music that your target market will remember and appreciate hearing, and therefore will listen to your ad.

If you want to sell to younger consumers, take to the social media "airwaves" with as many testimonials as you can generate, because that is where those people are hanging out. You want them to try and write reviews about your products and post them on their Instagram pages. You won't catch them on Facebook; as soon as their parents started posting pictures of them when they were five and "friending" all of their friends, they took off. Facebook is now far more the domain of Baby Boomers. Baby Boomers who own cats.

Here is the biggest take away—the rule for generational communication of your marketing message is that you have to change the content and the location of where you place your messages in order to reach them.

Our marketing messages are properly skewed generationally.
○ YES   ○ NO, we have corrections to make.

We have a great handle on how we market to different generations.
○ YES   ○ NO

14

Written Communications Your English Teacher Would Love

I am going to make an assumption that if you are reading a marketing book, you are looking for ways to improve your marketing efforts. One of those improvements is to use written communications through social media to connect with people we have not met in person. I would like to postulate that marketing done correctly promotes your best side. It shows your best face to the world. Proper use of language in your written communications is the key to this part of your marketing effort. The week I wrote this chapter, I received three letters through LinkedIn that did not do any of the senders any favors toward making a positive impression. In fact, only one of them received a return email from me.

In LinkedIn, I have about fifteen hundred connections, roughly one third of whom I have not met. When I get a new request, I take a look at their profile and send them my standard response. I use a couple of standard responses because, A) it is easy, and B) to just hit "yes" in response to the connection is not helping me begin to build a relationship with my connections.

Here is my first standard response:

> Hi (insert first name)! Thank you for connecting with me on LinkedIn. I follow my Facebook pages more frequently so it may be a good idea for you to Like my www.Facebook.com/SedonaMarketingRetreats page, and Friend me up at www.Facebook.com/hankyuloff. At the SMR page you will get a constant stream of marketing tips and on the Hank Yuloff page you will get a constant stream of . . . well . . . me. Friend me up and let me know what a good referral to you would be so I will recognize an opportunity for you when I see it!
> Thanks again,
>   Hank
>   (800)705-4265 FREE
> P.S. (I share something which might resonate with them based on their profile.)

The second one:

> Thanks so much for connecting with me. I want to reach out to you to say "Howdy" and learn more about you.
>
> I took a quick look at your profile and I would like to know more about you and your professional background. Since I do a lot of networking and referring business, are you open to a quick phone call or cup of coffee?
>
> By the way, how is LinkedIn working for you in helping you grow your business? I'm very knowledgeable about that platform (and Facebook, too) and might have a few suggestions for you to improve your results after we talk.
> Once again thanks for the connection. I hope to hear from you soon.
> All the best,
> Hank Yuloff

Notice how even in my written communications I am letting my personality show through, while remaining professional. No typos. No fractional sentences.

I want to share three letters I have received through the LinkedIn email system. Each person had sent me a connection request and received my standard response. I have not altered anything other than taking out their name.

Hello hank,
Thanks for reaching out to me. I'd be interested in setting up a call. I'm curious though, are you just looking too add a graphic designer to your professional network or are you just trying to sell me some advice. Because if that's the case (no offense) I'm not too interested.

Otherwise I'd be glad to share a few things about my profession and possibly hear a few things about yours. I'm highly fascinated with marketing and I'm sure you are too.
Sender first name only

Hi Hank,
Please keep (company name)'s services in mind for clients in 2015.
(Company Name) partners with small businesses to manage
Human Resources, Benefits, Payroll, etc. and ensure compliance
with California labor and employment laws.
Sender Name and Info

Hey Hank thanks for reaching out My professional background
is actually mostly Customer service but slowing building a UX
brand. I haven't really used LinkedIn to network most because of
laziness but currently on a 30 day goal of providing as much as
value as I can give to people and trying to figure out how to brand
my message of real world usability.
I am currently following M.S, T.L. and A.M. among others podcast
so maybe they can provide you some valuable knowledge.
You can call me almost any time (Phone)
Thank you,
Sender first and last name

Our lesson for this chapter is that when you send written communication, it should be solid. It should be something your high school English teacher would grade at a B or above level. This is especially true when you are communicating with someone new.

Remember the phrase, "You only get one chance to make a first impression," so take the time to make a good impression.

Here's another way to look at this. When I was a sales manager for a promotional products company, I had to interview hundreds of people each year. In order to narrow it down from the thousands of resumes I received, I had a process of elimination. Experience was one way, but bad cover letters and typographic errors were reasons for immediate elimination. Your letters or written connections through social media are a resumé asking for business or to be referred. Make them count.

The written transmission of our marketing missives are not arduously onerous for our audience.

◯ YES ◯ NO

15

Know Your Target Market, Bob-Dylan Style

Bob Dylan sure knows his audience! But is he targeting them properly?

An article from the CNN Money website is about Bob Dylan offering a free album to AARP members.*

Bob Dylan is now almost seventy-five years old, and his target market is in that same age range, plus or minus twenty years. That group grew up with vinyl and easily made the transition to using CDs. Many of us even re-purchased most of our favorite albums in that platform. Dylan's *Shadows in the Night* album (his first since 2012) is a gift arriving by mail to a random selection of fifty thousand of AARP's thirty-five million subscribers.

Since Dylan was still touring when I wrote this, this is a great way to A) let his audience know he has a new album out, B) generate interest in seeing him live, and C) generate album sales to those who read articles about the giveaway and know it exists.

Why would you give away your product to your target market? Because sometimes it makes good sense. I have given free marketing plans to non-profits referred to me through different networking groups to which I belong. This has not only made me feel good, but it generates business for me from people who want to support what I do for non-profits. In the case of Dylan, he gave away fifty thousand albums to people in his target market, and others in that target market now know it is time to go buy a new Dylan album. It is also safe to say that many of those fifty thousand will be listening to their first Dylan album and become fans.

Take an inventory of the products and services you offer. Is there some service or product that *you* can offer to a limited section of your target market that will benefit you through publicity? If there is, make sure you do not keep it a secret. This is when public relations directed at your target market can come in handy.

I love Bob Dylan.

◯ YES   ◯ NO, but I would if I could understand the words.

*(http://money.cnn.com/2015/01/25/retirement/bob-dylan-free-album/index.html?source=yahoo_hosted)

16

Marketing Tips to Improve Sales in a Retail Store

It is sometimes difficult for neighborhood retail businesses to improve sales and solidify a marketing plan, especially one that will work all the time. This is because at different times of the year certain retail neighbors in that neighborhood can affect their business in ways over which they have very little control. For example, what if you had a neighbor in your retail center that sold Christmas trees for six weeks of the year, affecting the traffic in your parking lot.

If you are the lucky owner of one of these establishments, I thought I would share a few tips to help improve sales and build a better relationship with your top clients.

1. Create a Preferred Buying Club. This can be a by-invitation-only proposition, or have your customers self-select. By keeping track of sales by client, you can easily decide which clients are in your top 20% and offer them special services. It could be a concierge service for your company, members-only sales, or other preferred methods of communicating with you.

2. Create a mailing list. And when I say mailing list, I mean *mailing*, not an e-mail list. Open and response rates for emails are not what they were even a couple of years ago so to improve sales you better create a list where you can get your message into your client's hands. Designing an incredible mailer is difficult, but for a retail business, the better the special, the more effective the response will be. Here is my best example: How far would you go out of your way for a 10% discount on a burger and fries lunch? How about if I give you 50% off—or two for one? If you want some tips on developing this list, keep reading or give us a call.

3. Ask your customers to sell out their friends for a discount. Tell them that if they refer a friend to your company, both your customer and their friend will get some incredible special. This is a great way to

improve sales because referrals make for the best customers. I think I will do this to improve sales for my business right now: If you and a friend are both new clients to Promotionally Minded and order promotional products from us, you will each get a 20% discount on your first orders.

4. While you are grabbing your customer's mailing addresses, you can ask them to opt in for a once a month text marketing special. Send them an awesome special and you will have them looking *forward* to your texts! Do not abuse this very personal connection your client has given to you.

If you have not created a mailing list, but still want to use direct mail, the U.S. Postal Service has a service called Every Door Direct Marketing which allows you to break down your geographic mailings by letter carrier. Their website has very specific directions, so check them out for the rules.

We have several ways to build our mailing list.
○ YES   ○ NO

Two Cases of Direct Mail Done Incorrectly

We received two very bad pieces of direct mail done incorrectly in just three days. Let's take a look at these pieces of direct mail and see how to avoid repeating their mistakes.

Bad Direct Mail Exhibit A

According to Country's economy problems we try to be helpful to our customers and we offer low prices for your POOL or SPA service. You well make a wise decision if you use our offer and you well save a lot and most of your money. Please call this number and we will try to save your POOL or SPA cleaning with low prices. Remember we think and always worry for our customers. (818)468-16-26. Or email artyomohanyan@yahoo.com

Sincerely – ART.

ART'S POOL SERVICE
Swimming Pool & Spa service & repair

pool & spa water cleaning,service, fix or repair

10531 Oxnard st. North Hollywood
CA 91606

(818)468-1626
artyomohanyan@yahoo.com

This sales solicitation letter came to us in a handwritten envelope— with just our address. The return address was imprinted in a perfectly acceptable way using a rubber stamp, *but* had the phone number written the same way as in the letter with an extra dash.

Clearly this was produced by someone who does not have strong written English skills. But for those of us who *do*, the lesson is pretty clear: Have people look at the sales pieces you want to mail out before you spend the money to send them. If it is your business, take pride in it no matter what you do for a living and show your professionalism. In this case, it makes me think that if I have questions or comments, will I be able to effectively communicate with Art? And if price is the main selling point of Art's service, what corners is he cutting to get that price down?

Bad Direct Mail Exhibit B

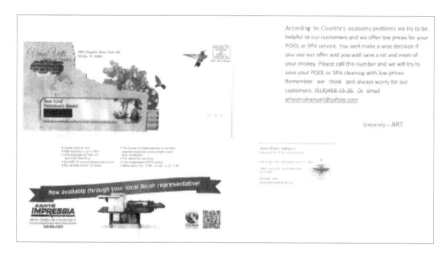

The other piece of direct mail done incorrectly was this envelope (two, actually, addressed differently so it cost the advertiser twice as much) that appears to be sent from a home and garden shop. On the other side is an ad for a copier company. On one of the two envelopes this second side was misprinted at an angle. A very confusing piece of direct mail even before we get inside the envelope.

Oh, and there was nothing inside the envelope. They were empty. This isn't direct mail done incorrectly, it's direct mail done stupidly.

Direct mail is more than just making a wild a$$ guess. To do it exceptionally is very hard. But to not do it incorrectly, is much easier.

This chapter is discussed more completely at the beginning of our radio show: The Marketing Checklist! You can find the show at www.OurMarketingchecklist.com.

We do direct mail properly.

◯ YES   ◯ NO, we need a refresher course.

18

Custom URLs—the Vanity License Plates of the Internet

"What's in a name? That which we would call a rose,

By any other name would smell as sweet . . ."
—Juliette in *Romeo and Juliette* by William Shakespeare

Let's talk about one of the most important identifiers our business uses—the name of our Uniform Resource Locator, or URL. It's the way people find our website on the internet.

Most companies have just one URL—the name of their company, and sometimes that name is quite long. Had I not started Promotionally Minded before the explosion of the internet the corporate name would be much shorter. In fact, if OurMarketingGuy.com did not have such a familiar OMG acronym, we would be using a different URL. For our work in Arizona, we have the vanity URLs SedonaOMG.com and SedonaPromos.com reserved.

A little while ago, I was handed a pen with a vanity URL on it. It was a great descriptive phrase for her business instead of the company name. A of couple weeks later, I needed to get in touch with that woman. I typed in the URL to grab her phone number and found out that it was, for lack of a better term, out of service. She had let it go. When I finally tracked down her phone number I asked her about the URL. She said that she was only going to use her company name and that this other one "wasn't worth the upkeep."

Upkeep. For $15 a year, she let go of a vanity URL filled with terms people search for when looking for her industry. A $15 bit of insurance was keeping her from getting more business—and who knows how many other people were using that pen, and were now thinking that she was out of business because the URL is gone. Or worse yet, what if that bit of on-line real estate were grabbed by a competitor.

That *is* what the internet is: virtual real estate. And is it better to rent real estate or own it?

So what are the best ways to design a vanity URL? Here are three of them. First, you can use geographic indicators—for example, we reserved www.SFVAcupuncture.com for our client, an acupuncture special-ist. It's a lot shorter than his clinic name and will generate a lot better organic search engine optimization because a lot of people will type in location and type of service when looking for his type of service. In the same way, we own www.ValleyPromotionalProducts.com because people who type in those terms to find promotional products in the San Fer-nando Valley find Promotionally Minded.

Second, it's also great to use vanity URLs for affiliate links. For our Send-OutCards business, when someone is looking to start a business, we use www.IDeserveItAll.com to direct people who want more out of life to our oppor-tunity site. When someone does not like their boss, or I truly want to make them laugh, we use www.GodIHateMyBoss.com to go to the same place. Both of them are easy to remember.

We have a client, a business lawyer named Bob Epstein, who has the reg-ular URL for his law firm, but also has www.ItsAGreatDayToSue.com. It allows him to have a bit of humor while he takes care of his client's business.

Third, if you can capture the generic .guru or generic .com of your indus-try or product, you should. I own PromotionalProduct.guru, OurMarketing.guru, TheBlogging.guru, and several others. Now I hate being called a *guru*. I'm not. It's a term people use to describe you when they cannot figure out what great things to say. That being said—it is a great way to call attention to yourself.

Use a little bit of creativity and you too, can grab some extra real estate.

We have all the URLs we can handle.
○ YES   ○ NO, but we could use some help figuring them out.

19

The Magical Sales Triangle

Let's talk about the basic process of delivering services. There are three ways to deliver your product or service:

Incredible speed
Incredible quality
Incredible price

Ideally, you would like to deliver all three to every client, but unless you are the only company in your industry (for example, you are the only company who can actually use the word *energize* and have someone show up in moments on the other side of the continent) this is an impossibility. If you give the highest quality product, someone is going to knock you off at a lower price.

So given that we all have competition, we should decide which one or two of these "incredibles" we can deliver and merge them into our Unique Selling Proposition, which gives our sales effort a personality.

Here are nine tips to blend into your sales message:

1. Be attractive. Make your listeners want to hang out with you.

2. Create a better life or desire for it.

3. Become a person of character. Nothing worse than having a person say that he is "all in" on your deal and then you find out that he has lots of other deals going on which conflict.

4. Always be improving. This is one of the reasons that Sedona Marketing Retreats exists, to help our clients improve their message and their sales abilities.

5. Become relevant to the world. You must be a problem solver.

6. Become the link to solve the problem. If you are not taking away their pain of some sort, they are not writing you a check.

7. Appeal to the emotional side of people.

8. Build your credibility. Social proof or testimonials from your raving fans are vital.

9. Create significance and inclusion. People need to feel like they belong in your world. They are part of what is going on. They are in on the joke.

Our sales process is as magical as a unicorn.
◯ YES   ◯ NO, but we believe in unicorns.

20

Using Facts Not in Evidence, Your Honor

There are a bunch of cellular service companies where you can buy your unlimited minutes and data plan (until you get to a certain amount then we will slow down your service, right AT&T?) for your portable phone, camera, and internet accessing devices.

They are all providing the same service—delivering data to their customer.

The way they do it is through their network of wires, satellites, Wi-Fi, and just plain Keebler Elf magic that most of us do not understand nor care about as long as when we push the power button, it comes to life. Or as I put it when the hood of my car goes up: I have reached the end of my knowledge.

According to the previously discussed Sales Triangle, since the product speed is virtually the same, then they only have price or coverage.

But wait, are they all the same? The answer is *no*—and how they choose to represent that fact is awesome.

Most of the time, 95% of us use our devices only at home, at work, and in between the two. We are in the same fifty square mile area 90% of the time. This means that our coverage area—and the cell service we buy—should be the one that works the best in our area.

But these companies insist on showing us ads which compare their network to the rest of the United States. The simple question is, "What do I care how Verizon outperforms Sprint in Omaha if I will never be *going* to Omaha?" I want to know how it outperforms in the fifty-square-mile box I live and work in 90% of the time.

What the companies are trying to do is make you think that since they have better coverage than their competitors—or that they have a large coverage area where you live, that is more important than pricing because "you don't want to have your call dropped, do you?"

Their research shows that you are more concerned with having your important calls dropped than you are with a small price difference. And a map of the country will act as a marketing diversion.

So don't forget to check your plan every month, because they change constantly and you may be able to save some money.

Our advertisements are honest and designed to help our clients get the most out of our services.

◯ YES   ◯ NO

21

Hey Niches! You're My Favorite "Picture Niche!"

"All those who sell to everyone please raise your hand."

It's one of my favorite questions to ask when I am in front of an audience and want to talk about niching down your target market. I am coining a term here, and calling it a *picture niche*.

From the back, one hesitant, reticent hand went up and it made me so happy. Looks like we've got ourselves a demographic convoy!

I instantly accessed a conversation we had previously so, knowing where this conversation was going to go, I asked the woman in the back, "tell me what you do."

"I sell loans to home buyers."

I sell loans? In six words, she allowed me to put her into the demographic box that anyone whom she had just met, would put her in.

But, I asked, who is your *favorite* kind of client to work with?

"New and first time home buyers."

"So, someone buying their fourth house, in another state, would not be your target, right?"

"Well, no."

What happened here was an incredible sales person who got anxious to make every sale instead of doing more of the kind of business that she really wanted to write.

Rather than do that, what she should have done was made a list of the people she wanted to help and target her messages towards that picture niche:

- More the than half are married, less than 10 years and are age 25 to 35.
- Nine out of 10 are renters.
- They are mostly w-2 employees compared to entrepreneurs.
- Their combined incomes are close to $100,000+

When we go through a list of twenty or so demographic questions with our clients, we create a much clearer picture of who we want to talk to and how we want to create their messages for narrow-casted consumption.

Walmart may be the largest retailer in the United States but not everyone shops there. Coca Cola may enjoy a very loyal following, but so does Pepsi. Apple has developed a cult following with their products, but like everyone who has ever rooted for the Boston Red Sox knows, PC lovers and Yankee fans are just as ferocious in defending their brands as well. Don't try and convince a Sox fan to root for your Bronx Bombers—just make sure your message has lots of NYs in it. Niche it, baby!

Another example of this is my favorite personal avatar, Harriot, named for my grandfather, Harry.

Harriot is between forty and sixty-five, and is the right-hand woman of the man who owns the company. Generally, he is busy with the sales function, so Harriot is in charge of HR, accounting, and the marketing function. She is married and usually self-designates as Christian. Of the eight Harriots I have met in my career, five went to college and are all wicked smart. The last part is that any employee who crosses Harriot is gone pretty quickly because the owner knows how valuable and loyal she is to him. I have met her running a chain of private schools, a bank, and a variety of other business types.

When I meet a Harriot I know exactly how I am going to work with her and I change my sales function to "extreme information" because that is what I know she wants and appreciates from her vendors.

Get the picture?

What does *your* Harriot look like? How do you recognize her?

As an aside, Picture Niche Target Marketing is one of the reasons we are careful in choosing which social media platform we use when connecting with our target clients, because we want it to match where our clients hang out.

I'm going to help Hank Yuloff promote his concept of Picture Niche Target Marketing by developing my own picture of Harriot.
⃝ YES   ⃝ NO, I want to name mine something else.

22

The Absolute Bestest Amazingest Coolest Thing Ever!

At one time or another we have all said it—*all of us*: "I don't believe advertising."

And yet, we all buy things that are advertised. Interesting disconnect, huh?

I have always *loved* "Higher Ground" by Stevie Wonder. It is one of my go-to songs before I go on stage to make a presentation. It always puts me in an amazing mood. When it comes to music, it could be—the absolute bestest amazingest coolest thing ever!

But then I listen to"September" by Earth Wind and Fire and think that *that* song is the absolute bestest amazingest coolest thing ever!

The point is here *believability*. Advertising and its sisters, marketing and public relations, have gotten a bad rap (some of it entirely deserved) because of claims that could not be possible.

- The best thing since sliced bread.
- The Happieset Place on Earth.
- The Greatest Show on Earth.
- The Best Part of Waking Up, is Folger's in Your Cup. (Or Rockapella singing that jingle!)

As company owners we have to avoid hyperbole. It takes away from our credibility and will hurt the claims we make which *are* accurate. If a product is that good, we do not need to over-sell it. We want our value statements to be as accurate as possible.

The tip: Dial back the over-sell. In fact, if you *do* have the absolute bestest amazingest coolest thing ever, let your customers do the talking for you. The *buzz* will do it! Grab video testimonials whenever you can (video is better— see my blog on that).

Have you made positive changes in your product? Try this: "We have an improved product and we think you are going to like it. Here is what we have done. . . ."

Remember that there are other products and services which are similar to yours. Some of them could be better. But just because one film wins the

Oscar for best picture, it does not mean that the rest of the nominated films are not just as good. And just because one team wins the Super Bowl, it does not mean that another half dozen teams were not worth watching if you wanted to see a great football game.

Guarantees help you support your claims. Our Promotionally Minded Marketing Days comes with a 5-Star Guarantee. If you do not "star" at least five things in your workbook that are game changers, we give you your money back. I am backing up my claim that we put on an incredible event. There are lots of others who say that sort of thing from the stage, but we put it in writing. *Everywhere.*

Our product is the best, we just need help telling people.
◯ YES   ◯ NO, we have all the business we can handle.

23

Another Advertising Medium Goes Away

For years, when I have talked about how advertising media has changed, I have told people that if they want to learn how to sell, they should get a job hawking ad space for a direct mail weekly shopper called the *PennySaver*. The shopper had classified ads for garage sales, private-party used cars, rental homes, and various services as its editorial copy. That copy filled in the spaces around display ads for local restaurants, furniture stores, and dentists. A business could also stuff a flyer inside the eight by ten newsprint book and have them delivered right into every local mailbox in a geographic area. In other words, every column inch of the thing brought in revenue. The profits margins were huge.

With that in mind, imagine my surprise when I read that the Southern California version of the product had suddenly, without warning, closed its doors. According to the new CEO, installed in February, the publication was "forced to shut down after its lender unexpectedly ceased our funding."

Working for that type of company selling that kind of product puts a salesperson into a two-zip-code area, seeing the same retail business owners every week, sharing with them the benefits of having their message delivered directly into the mailboxes of their neighbors. Not every business *wants* that kind of demographic coverage, but retail businesses almost certainly do. The challenge is that most small, one-location retail business owners are consistently underfunded in the marketing department, so you had better be incredible at describing the benefits of your product and have lots of testimonials to back them up.

It is also an inexpensive way to send direct mail out to a geographic area where you want to do business. According to their website, the *PennySaver* was delivered to eleven million people weekly, though that includes a "pass along" equation of about 2.5 per household which I never believed and did not use.

As the *PennySaver* tries to regroup, we will see if it does come back as a printed edition. It seems like that business model should still work, unlike an age-old competitor, the *Yellow Pages* books, which have all but disappeared. If someone wants a plumber, they look them up online, but the *PennySaver* offers discounts and specials—more active advertising, which gives it extra value to its readers. The *Yellow Pages* model has attempted to morph into an online version but there really is no reason to go to a directory website when you can just type what you want in to a browser. The *Pennysaver* model, if they are willing to spend enough money to promote it, could serve as (yet another) place on the internet to go for coupons. My guess is that they will want to go the application route. But will people really *pay* to be on it? If I am having a garage sale, I can put it on CraigsList.com for free.

We are not using outdated modes of delivering our message.
◯ YES ◯ NO

24

The Trade Show Emergency Kit

It was three months after we moved, and we were preparing to exhibit at our first trade show in a new state. Over the years, I have gotten pretty good at setting those booths and tables up. It *is* part of my job! The trade show boxes had promotional product samples, which were always asked about: Do you do hats? Do you do pens? Do you do t-shirts? Do you do pens? Do you do . . . They had the table cloths with logos. They had sell sheets. They had giveaways. Next to the boxes, in the storage area, were our table-top banners and full-size banners. It was just a matter of pulling out the right things for the particular show where we were exhibiting.

I also had my magic-trade-show bag. In it, I had placed all the things we needed when setting up. All the things other exhibitors usually had left in their offices and came around looking for. Yes—when your best targets at a trade show are the other exhibitors, you want to have what they need.

In getting ready for this show, what I did not know that was that somewhere in the move, my magic-trade-show bag had disappeared.

So as I was putting together magic-trade-show bag #2, I thought I would share my list with you.

> Scissors
> Velcro
> String
> Sharpies (black, red, blue)
> Various tapes—duct, packing, scotch
> Extension cords
> Power strip
> Pens—with your logo
> Name badges with your logo
> Lanyards
> Box cutters
> Twist ties
> Sign hooks
> Bandages
> Aspirin (some pain reliever)
> Blank white paper for signs on the fly

Paper with your logo as a header
Stapler with a box of staples
Business cards
Batteries
Portable radio to listen to during set up
Wipe and write markers
Eraser
Copies of your book
Copies of *my* book
Basket for business cards
Giveaway box for people to drop their cards in to
Blank forms for people to put their info on.
Extra t-shirts in case you spill
Stain remover
Navy blue tie
Bungie cords
C hooks
Sign holder easel
Phone charger
Plastic bags
Shoe laces
Hand sanitizer
Super glue
Highlighters
Glue Stick
$50 in small bills
Rubber bands in a baggie.
Clothes steamer (for those of you who are truly picky)
Tennis shoes for break down

You should bring enough pens to drop one or two off at each of the other booths in case someone forgot theirs.

We have a trade show emergency kit.
◯ YES   ◯ NO, but we are putting it together.

25

You're Fired

Our company puts together marketing plans for businesses and I have been telling clients for the longest time that there are three categories of customers:

1. The top 5%—the kind of clients that don't necessarily make up the highest dollar amount, but the ones you most like to work with. When you see their phone number appear you are super excited. They don't necessarily make up the most sales; some of these clients could be small-dollar clients who refer you a ton of business. Most of these clients are unicorn-like because they do not come around very often and may not stick around, either. In sales we call them Blue Birds. When I began working in the promotional product business, one of my 5% clients was Disney. I sold them all of their playing cards for the Land, the World, and the Center. It was high volume, and a low commission, but the high volume made up for it. I also knew that it was not going to last more than a few years, and I was right: they were able to save a nickel a deck and started getting them overseas instead of American made.

2. The next 20%—the best clients that appreciate you, that are consistent and when you see their phone number show up on your phone you never hit "ignore." They are the high volume, high frequency buyers.

3. The next 60%—normal clients. The bulk of your clients who keep the lights on. In the promotional product world, the average order is about $1000 and these would be the $250-$1000 orders which come very steadily.

Notice the total is 85%.

I tell clients that the bottom 15% of your clients, are the ones who should be fired. They are the ones who take the most time and never appreciate you. They pay late and approach you with the attitude that they are your best clients. These are the clients that, if you said goodbye to them, you could spend more time developing your relationship with the 60% clients and turning them in to 20% clients and turning your 20% clients into the 5% clients.

Firing a client is the healthiest thing you can do for your business. And it feels *great*.

We have a plan to turn our 60%ers into 20%ers and 20%ers into 5%ers.
◯ YES ◯ NO

26

I'm Sorry! Here, Have a Free T-shirt

For years, when explaining to a group the usefulness of promotional products, I have asked, "How many of you have done something (like run a 5k) and the deciding factor was that you got a free t-shirt? Or you bought something because they had a free imprinted something like a travel mug or umbrella included in the purchase?"

The organizers of the Standard Chartered Bangkok Half-Marathon must had been at one of my speaking engagements because to make up for a mistakenly laid out course, they gave the runners a free t-shirt as an apology gift. The mistake was not in the runner's favor, it was an extra four miles (seven kilometers).

"No *wonder* my time was off!" was the most often heard comment by the six thousand runners who were in the November 17, 2015 race.

Songkram Kraison, vice president of the Jogging Association of Thailand explained that "Even those who didn't finish—will get a special jersey to wear like a badge of pride."

He's right. Those special t-shirts have a much higher perceived value than the shirt itself because of what is imprinted on it. Many of us have t-shirts which have seen much better days but we keep them because of what is *printed* on them. A concert, an event, a brand we strongly relate to, a sports team, our school, a trip we took can all make us think instantly of a happy memory. Sharyn and I just ran (well, we walked, actually, and I had a cup of coffee in my hand the entire way) a 5k at Disneyland with ourSendOutCards team and the t-shirts we wore will continue to remind us of our 5 a.m. jaunt through part of the Magic Kingdom. The same can be said for many promotional products. At Promotionally Minded, we have sold embroidered caps, jackets, medals, pins, and even pens and portfolios which carried the special logo of an event. It is one of the best uses of promotional products.

The Jogging Association of Thailand summed up their free t-shirt gift by saying "The T-shirt is meant to "express our admiration for your spirit in bravely overcoming the obstacles."

Just remember not to assume you know what and how to make it right. Apologize, but ask the other person what they feel will "make things right."

Have options ready, but don't offer them first. Focus on what comes next and remember that time may heal, but action accelerates it.

Our company policy when an order goes south is that we will replace the product at no charge, no questions asked. This policy arose out of working for a competitor that required everything short of a blood test before handling a challenge.

We have a policy for what happens in the event of a mistake.
◯ YES   ◯ NO, and I'm sorry about that.

27

No One Wants to Look at Boobs Anymore?

One of three biggest lies told by men—"I only read Playboy for the articles"—finally came true. After over sixty years, *Playboy* announced, the same month in which we published the first edition of this book, that it was making a major marketing change and no longer going to put pictures of naked women in its magazine. . . . Kind of like Budweiser not putting alcohol in its beer—what's the point of drinking that crap if you are not going to get a buzz. What's the point of *Playboy* without pictures of beautiful, surgically-altered, and airbrushed naked women to . . . enjoy.

Why are they taking away our bottomless bunnies? There must be some marketing manifestation, right? Yes.Money. Money is the reason for the major marketing change. *Playboy's* rack sale (pardon the pun) circulation has dropped from 5.6 million copies a month during the 1970s to roughly 850,000 in today's world. And with good reason, I guess. Whereas when I grew up, having a *Playboy* magazine (or it's more lewd counterpart, *Hustler*) in the drawer always provided *risqué* entertainment for teenage boys—you had to be eighteen to buy those magazines. Now, we live in a world where if one wants porn, all you have to do is type whatever sexual behavior you are interested in viewing into the internet browser and it is delivered to you—ranked by how many other people found it to be awesome.

CEO of *Playboy,* Scott Flanders, agreed with me when he said, "You're now one click away from every sex act imaginable for free. And so it's just passé at this juncture." The magazine will still feature a Playmate of the Month (and therefore the Playmate of the Year), but they will be rated PG-13, which probably means, no nipple. Kind of like Maxxim—all the titillation with the actual . . . you get the point.

How will this make them more money? The Playboy website has already been made more acceptable for younger viewers, resulting in younger readers, which gives them an increase in web traffic, where they can sell more ads.

The chief content officer of the magazine, Cory Jones, said *Playboy* will be "more accessible and more intimate." He also said, and I agree with the first part, "Twelve-year-old me is very disappointed in current me. But it's the right thing to do."

I do have a bit of a personal worry. For the last thirty years, I have sold *Playboy* calendars with my client's ads on them through our promotional products division, Promotionally Minded. I wonder if that means that they are going away soon, too. The 2016 versions are already created, so stay tuned for the 2017 editions.

Playboy founder Hugh Hefner, age eighty-nine, has agreed with the proposal to stop publishing images of naked women after the March 2016 edition. So get your grubby hands ready boys—it is going to be a collector's item.

I only read Hank's books and blog for the articles.
◯ YES ◯ NO

28

Catch the Wave—An Artist's Story

We were able to catch the wave the other day, figuratively. Our assistant, Blaine, had just joined Sharyn, and I in Sedona to set up the office forSedona Marketing Retreats and I thought it would be a good idea to take everyone out to breakfast. "It's time for all of you to taste the best bread pudding—*ever*," I said.*

So off we went to Sedona Sweet Arts for bread pudding and coffee. While we were sitting down and going through the game plan for the day, I saw a man trying to decide what to have with his coffee.

"Go for the bread pudding," I said.

"Huh?" he said.

"The bread pudding. It will be the highlight of your day."

From there, the conversation began. His name is Jack Nordby and he was visiting Sedona from Maui, Hawaii to find outlets for his metal-etched art. He said his rental car had just turned itself into the parking lot and here he was standing there sharing with us about how he had created his first piece of art, and the road that had taken him to Arizona. During our conversation, Jack explained how he was sitting on the beach in Maui and while watching the waves crash in, realized that he could recreate their action in metal in such a way that the motion of the waves would be captured. It was a fascinating story, about how he could catch the wave in metal, and it was one that I knew I could help him tell.

Then my marketing A.D.D. kicked in and we started talking about his logo, his sales materials (oh dear, don't *tell* me you got them from that online printing company instead of using a graphic artist), and his plans for the future.

From that discussion, we began to form a friendship, and we continued our conversations. The following Friday we got to see some of Jack's work.

* In chapter twenty-one I admonished to be very careful of hyperbole and then here I am saying that the bread pudding is the best ever . . . *wow*! It is true, though.

Check out our website blog for videos of his amazing art. Here's hoping that this is the beginning of a long business and personal relationship. You never know when you can catch a wave—be open to the opportunities.

I am always open to beginning a conversation with a stranger.
◯ YES ◯ NO

29

The Video's the Thing

"You oughta be in pictures!" "He has a face for radio." "Smile! You're on *Candid Camera*."

With the advent of electronic image capture instead of film, the use of video in marketing has become more and more important. Whether you know it or not, or are willing to accept it or not, video has become a tremendous part of the marketing recipe.

Here are all the reasons to use it:

- They take almost no time to make
- They drive visitors to your websites
- They build links to other websites
- They build your authority on a subject
- Most of your competitors are afraid to use video, too. But unlike you, they are unwilling to learn to get past it!

Depending on the day, YouTube is one of the largest search engines in the world, and ignoring this reach is a detriment to your business. Besides, the web is a competitive place and if you use video, you leap past your competitors. YouTube also carries a built in authority, which, if coupled with the right competitive key words and phrases, can get your message placed right in front of the correct eyeballs—your ideal clients.

So how do you make videos? You can use a video camera, but your smartphone can be just as effective. The cameras have gotten better and better and let's face it, the device is always within ten feet of you and is incredibly easy to use. You can also use slide shows, animation, charts, PowerPoint . . . just add your voice-over and you're ready.

Here is an important tip: Keep your videos backed up on your hard drive. Do not keep the only copy on YouTube or any other website or service that you do not own and control.

Here is another important tip: If the thing that stops you from using video for your marketing is that you hate how you look or sound—or hate how you *think* you look or sound, then it is time to *get past it*. You look how you look. You sound like you sound. And none of us will ever sound like James Earl Jones, Barry White, or (my favorite when she does a southern accent) Meg Tilly.

Here is yet another important tip: Shorter is better, but take the time you need in order to get your message across. You should use these videos to introduce your blogs, your websites, on your landing pages, and everywhere else you appear on the internet.

As you do more video, I think you might find that you begin to enjoy it. That will be about the same duration of time when you will see them make your overall marketing plans more effective.

Our company constantly looks for ways to use video in our marketing.
◯ YES　◯ NO, but I'm ready for my close up!

30

Your Unique Selling Proposition—a Short, Sweet Elevator Ride to Success

This chapter is only for the entrepreneurs. If you are not entrepreneurial in nature, if you don't own a company, if you are not starting a company, then move on to the next chapter.

I want to talk about Unique Selling Propositions—USPs. The reason I want to talk about them is based on a couple of recent meetings that I had.

The question came up with a guy I was talking to: "So, what do you do?"

His answer was, "I'm an accountant." And by doing that he put himself in a box. Or he allowed someone who did not know what he did, *put* him in a box. He allowed *me* to decide what an accountant does.

To put it simply: Don't do that!

What I want you *to* do is come up with a ten- to fifteen-second elevator speech. If you can boil it down to just a few words, that's even better.

Here are a few examples of some great ones:

> The Happiest Place on Earth—Disneyland
> Just Do It—Nike
> The King of Beers—Budweiser
> We Try Harder—Avis (National would beg to differ!)
> What's In Your Wallet—Capital One

I use a couple of different USPs: "We help you keep the clients you have and find the clients you deserve or desire." If I know what the other person does, if I have been able to ask them what they do first, I tell them to think of their best clients. Then I say that I help them get more of that type of client.

Another USP—"Our Plans Depend on Yours," which speaks to clients who need a marketing plan and tells them that we are not a cookie-cutter marketing company.

We want to narrow down what someone thinks of us. I can say that we provide perfect promotional product ideas, or logo design, or a marketing plan, but those are the *features* of what I do. They are not the *benefits* of what I provide to my clients.

What are the features of what you do? What are the benefits? We want to mention the features, but focus on the benefits. We want people to get a clear picture in their mind of what you can do for them.

That is your USP—your Unique Selling Proposition. It's what sets you apart and makes you stand out when they think of your business category.

Since the third chapter of this book, we have already refined our USP.
◯ YES   ◯ NO, I am still working on it.

31

10+2 More Great Uses for Promotional Products

In *The Marketing Checklist: 80 Simple Ways to Master Your Marketing*, I covered 10+1 great ways to use promotional products. New book. New list. Last time we discussed product types in general and distribution plans, this time I am adding some specific products and their distribution plans into the mix.

1. **I am a calendar — use me as a fund raiser.** Many organizations use candy or products like wrapping paper as fund raisers. While these have been tried and true money raisers, they have a couple of faults which make them a hard sell. First, the prices are generally a lot higher than buying at retail, so the buyer is expected to know that they are definitely donating money. In other words, from a strictly product basis, they are not getting their normal money's worth. Second is that the profit margin is good, but not great.

   Calendars (with your ad on them) wonderfully solve both these problems:
   - They can have many themes—children, Norman Rockwell, pets, scenic, going green, motivational, etc.
   - Financially, they make sense. Let's say you want to make $3,000 from your next fund raiser. If you use calendars for fund-raising, 1,000 calendars will cost about $3.00 each. If you sell the calendars for just $9.00 (*this is below retail costs which average $10-15*), you make about a 300% profit. Raise the price by $1 and you are still at retail value and will make even more! To make that same $3,000, you would have to sell about 6,000 candy bars. Order calendars now, we will have them available in the fall, they can be sold immediately, and you will have your money before the bill is due.
   - By carrying your organization's name and other information the purchaser will be constantly aware of the group that he/she is supporting. The calendar will constantly be seen and used, thanking the purchaser for supporting your programs. At no charge, we can add first aid information or other custom info on the back!
   - For future fund raising: If you instruct everyone who sells the

catalog to write down the names and addresses of the people they sell to, you can develop a mailing list of supporters to be solicited in later years. You then send a letter and order form which says, "It's calendar time for (organization). We thank you for supporting us in the past and hope you have enjoyed our calendars so much that we can count on your support now. This year we offer (calendar description). Simply mail this back and we will return the calendar to you."

- There is a *free* insert page that can carry the information about your school or organization on the inside.
- There is an opportunity to sell an ad on the calendar to a another business who wishes to sponsor it—making *more* money for your organization.

2. **Get on someone else's table, event, or stage.** When you know of someone who is holding a seminar, offer to provide the pens or the notepads for their event. I have also sponsored (provided) the bags for a chamber of commerce business expo. That way everyone who comes in, gets my bag. (This is fantastic advertising—everyone is walking around with your name and people see it everywhere.) You may be able to negotiate a sponsorship in exchange for the giveaways you provide. Another business expo or event giveaway that is needed by the organizer are lanyards. Offer to put their logo, alternating with your logo. You can get all of these things, great lanyards, bags, pads, or pens for under $2 each.

3. **OK folks, I am going to share something in public I have never shared before.** *Only* my clients know this one. When it comes to promotional products, we want them to be memorable. Couple that with the most common promotional product — pens. How do we put the two things together — most common, yet memorable? We have to make the common special. I am not talking about giving out an expensive pen (though it was a Cross pen set that put me on my career path), it is about making the pens you give out memorable. How about if the pen was magic?

   Here are two ways I make that ubiquitous little tool special:
   - When I hand a pen to someone, I tell them that it is a "*magic pen*. It is 100% guaranteed to never make a mistake. . . . (pause for reaction) Well, if you don't." It generally gets a smile. I continue with

"if it ever makes a mistake call the number on the pen and I will replace it for free." This tells them that my phone number is on the pen; they now should have it implanted in their memory that they know how to get in touch with me.

- One of the pens that I give out has three side — it is a triangle barrel. On one side, I have imprinted "Earthquake Detector." Living in an area where the ground can shake, this creates an instant connection. If I am in the client's office, I offer to "install it" and then put it on one of their shelves (where it is always in view to them and guests in their office). If I meet them out of the office, I offer to come by and install it. There is an extra part of this story. Years ago, I was doing business with Disney, selling them all of their playing cards. After the December 1988 quake in Pasadena, I had received a call from my contact at the company who let me know that in her 10x10 windowless office, all of the Disney plush toys that lined the walls, shelf after shelf, had fallen off their places, but she found my Earthquake Detector at the bottom, so she assumes that if she had been in the office at 3:30 in the morning when the earthquake hit, she would have seen that pen fall off first.

4. **Get stuck on magnets.** We have several types of automotive-body repair clients who use magnets in the shape of a bandage. All of their employees were given a stack of them. When they see a car with a boo-boo, they leave a bandage on the car. They say, "We can fix this boo-boo," and they offer a discount. The employees use a Sharpie to put their initials on the magnet side and get a spiff if one of their "patients" comes through the door.

5. **I have always felt that a promotional product has to be useful and needed.** Over the years, however, I think some products usefulness are just to make the recipient laugh and have a good time. Let's talk about a couple of them. Yo-yos are one. People love to play with them. Cowbells are another. The sound of the *clanger* clanging while people hear Christopher Walken saying, "I need more cowbell," makes them smile and associate a smile with your name. And a smiling client is a happy client.

6. **I previously mentioned a t-shirt project as a way of discussing the message that appeared on the shirt.** I have had hundreds of

clients use wearables to promote their message, but I want to share something important. We would all love to have our clients wear our logo when they are out and about, but there must be a reason they would wear it. They have to relate to our message on the shirt. If they do not, they will not wear it. By example, there are fans of Harley Davidson motorcycles who would not only wear clothing with the Harley logo, but would go so far as to tattoo the logo on their bodies. A little less dramatic would be the choice of Coca Cola versus Pepsi. If you are a fan of one of those products, you may not emblazon your body with the logo, but you would probably wear a cool shirt with the stylized logo of the one you preferred. I just gave $10 to a non-profit in Phoenix for a shirt Coke had donated to them with a positive message that had the unique Coke bottle shape as well. I would not have done that with a Pepsi logo.

Similar strong product Hatfield-and-McCoy favoritism has existed between drivers of Chevy trucks and Ford trucks. Our assistant says she is a Ford Girl and she would never be caught wearing a Chevy cap. I don't care strongly about either (though I used to own a Ford Ranger) and would not wear either cap.

I don't think I need to even discuss sports team allegiances and their clothing. So what will people wear? If they are part of an organization, they will undoubtedly want to let others know they are part of that group. Compare that to, say, OurMarketingGuy.com. If I want people to wear my logo, I have to send it along in a subtle manner (a small logo on the bottom of the shirt, toward the side, so it can be tucked into a pair of jeans).

The message: Before you go to the expense of using wearables, make sure you know who is going to wear it and that you have a strong enough message and brand name that people will wear it.

7. **The only ads that get passed along if one person does not like it.** How many times have you seen an ad in a newspaper or in your mailbox or in your e-mail inbox that you eagerly passed along to someone else? While most ads are seen by one person, a promotional product has enough gift value that it can be re-gifted to someone else. Unlike an ad, if someone gets a flashlight, an umbrella, a flash drive that they cannot use, they will pass it along. This gives your ads another chance to pass on your message. The Advertising Specialty Institute has done studies which show that 62% of people who

receive a promotional product that they will not use, will give that item away before throwing it out.

8. **The Law of Reciprocity — Giving Often Leads to Receiving**. Quite often, giving a gift often promotes the feeling that a reciprocation is in order for the gesture. With promotional products, the research shows that 52% of participants who are given a promotional item, ultimately did business with that company. The other 48% of participants said they would be more likely to buy in the future. Using promotional products as that door opener can certainly help break the ice.

9. **Give a Certificate of Incredibleness!** We have awarded our clients and vendors for great service, being a Top 10 Client, and for being incredible. These awards can be plaques, but certificates can be just as effective. If it is a certificate, we like it to be a foil embossed (most of the certificate is foil which has been compressed into the paper) into card stock. We also have created different certificates that use our SendOutCards system (www.CardsByHank.com) to deliver. It takes up the 5x7 panel inside the card and uses variable printing so we can send out several at a time.

10. **A Small Measure of Maximum Marketing**. I have several clients who have needed something easy to mail *and* carry to a trade show *and* be useful in an office *and*, of course, does not cost a lot. Simple—a 7-inch clear light plastic ruler. About as close to perfectly practical and universally acceptable promotional product there is, outside of a pen. It is one of those products that everyone seems to have a place for and has high thank you, it's-just-what-I-needed value. In an envelope, it rattles around just enough, while not making the cost go up because the thickness of the envelope does not go beyond the minimum acceptable for first-class postage.

10+1. **Tech Protectors.** Whether it is a pouch, or a high-grade microfiber cloth, this class of products has skyrocketed to popularity in the past several years. It has been in an almost inverse relationship to another tech product, the mousepad. People will *always* enjoy another cloth (heavier ones for the car and computer bag, lighter ones for pocket or purse) to clean their screens. The advent of better mice and the popularity of laptops and tablets has made the pads, and almost by association, wrist rests, plummet in universal usefulness.

10+2. For one more, bonus way of using promotional products, check out the last chapter of the book!

Hokey smokes, those were great ideas!
○ YES   ○ NO, because we are not using them to promote *us* yet.

32

UCLA Athletics Market Their Ass Off— Like the Yankees

The world of sports often gives us subjects to talk about that relate back to our own marketing. Keeping in mind that your story—the things people can relate to about your company—is an important intangible in your success. The New York Yankees and the University of California Los Angeles had recent failures in being able to improve the narrative that is their tradition.

On the second day of the 2015 Major League Baseball draft, the New York Yankees had a chance to get their fan base excited by drafting and signing Mariano Rivera, Jr., the son of Hall of Famer-to-be Mariano Rivera to play in pinstripes. In the fourth round of the draft, the Washington Nationals took the ex-Bronx Bomber's pitching prodigy, losing the opportunity to continue the Rivera line in New York.

His father said that there was, "No disappointment. This is business. We treat it like that."

In the past few years, teams promoting their prospects bubbling up through the minor leagues is one of the ways they sell tickets. Lots of tickets. Having The Sandman's son in the fold and on the way, would build the legacy of the storied baseball team.

How does that relate to our businesses?

Let me use events as an example. My chamber of commerce has held an annual street faire for twenty-nine years. The story of how it came about, and the fact that neighbors look forward to it, is part of the story of the neighborhood. Some local commercial realtors promote the three-block footprint of the event to business owners who are looking to relocate to the area.

Similarly, our Promotionally Minded Marketing Days has become a part of our company's story. I am introduced all the time to people as the marketing person in the chamber who puts on events designed to help entrepreneurs with their marketing. People I meet also say to me, "I know you, you're the one who does those Ok, Late-Night Facebooker's questions every night on Facebook."

In other sports-marketing news, Let's head over to the west Los Angeles campus of UCLA. There was a chance that singer P. Diddy was going to be charged with a felony after *allegedly* confronting UCLA strength coach Sal

Alosi and a member of the UCLA staff with a kettlebell work-out weight.

From the *Los Angeles Times*: "Ricardo Santiago, a spokesman for the Los Angeles County district attorney's office, said prosecutors declined to file felony charges related to his June 22 arrest. The case was referred to the Los Angeles city attorney to decide whether Combs' conduct amounts to a misdemeanor. The prosecutors received the case Tuesday."

From the marketing world: When I first discussed Diddy's son getting a football scholarship, I said it was of no consequence if the kid was a starter as long as the team got photos of his dad wearing UCLA gear to promote to the world. This is the photo that, if I was a UCLA football coach, I would include in *every* recruiting package that got sent out to a high school prospect. The message? Come to UCLA—hang with Diddy. Oh, and did we mention? You'll probably meet *Snoop Dog*, too!

Does this little . . . what word to use here . . . *dust up* with a coach make a difference? Nope. The kid is a junior and barely playing so it's not going to affect team chemistry. And here is another photo for the UCLA marketing machine.

The lesson? Get pictures of your product with famous people. Get attached to them. Use that celebrity to promote *your* business. Sharyn and I are appearing in a video series that also stars Brian Tracy, one of the all-time best sales trainers. You think we are not using the photos we have with him? Only for the rest of our lives.

We realize the benefit of celebrity to promote our business.
◯ YES   ◯ NO, but I *am* a celebrity in my field.

33

Setting Your Marketing Calendar to Take Action on Time

Let our advance worrying become advance thinking and planning.
Winston Churchill

Never look back unless you are planning to go that way.
Henry David Thoreau

*Developing the plan is actually laying out the sequence of events
that have to occur for you to achieve your goal.*
George L. Morrisey

This is how to set your marketing calendar—work backwards so you hit all the deadlines to make your activities go off on time.

As part of a workshop I did for the Encino Chamber of Commerce, I discussed creating a marketing calendar as an important part of the marketing plans we put together. Since we all have (or should have) multiple marketing programs to move our message forward at one time, it is important to track in advance what needs to be done.

We have a tremendous number of programs available to us in order to market our business. They come in the technological form—things like email marketing, website and sales funnels; and they come in the traditional form—things like mail, radio, and networking. When we take any of these methods and prepare to use them to market our business, there are ways to make them more effective.

For example, if you are going to a trade show, you have to order promotional products, send clients direct mail pieces inviting them to stop by your booth, plan brochures and staffing, get the post trade show mailer prepared, and design the look of the booth. In other words, picking up a stack of pamphlets an hour before the show opens and heading down to the convention center does not constitute a plan for success.

The same goes for every tactic. If you are going to blog twice a week, you can figure out how long it is going to take you and how far in advance you have to begin writing it.

At holiday time, who is in charge of getting the holiday cards out? That person needs to be given a list of names and addresses way in advance of the mailing day. Most companies have to go through a printer, so that takes a week or so, so back that up. We use, and sell, an online system called Send-OutCards that allows us to capture addresses during the year. We can then send out a thousand holiday cards in about two hours. One hour to design the card, and another to just check off names. SendOutCards prints, stuffs, stamps, and mails them within twenty-four hours of us entering the information into our account. And they are *a lot* less expensive than the cards we used to have printed. And we do not have to pay our staff to sit there and stuff, lick stamps, and add labels. You can try it for free at www.CardsByHank.com.

In putting together your yearly plan, start with a blank calendar—I suggest a wall calendar or something you can print. Get everyone in the company involved because you never know what little part of the project might get forgotten. For example, if your assistant is in charge of ordering the promotional products from Promotionally Minded for every trade show you attend, and he is not let in on a new show that you are trying, those products may be late.

It is never too early to start planning your calendar for the next year. You will make some changes as you go, but it is a great feeling to know that you have your entire team pulling together to make your sales efforts more successful.

We have a marketing calendar set at the beginning of each year.
◯ YES   ◯ NO

34

Spelling Counts, Young Man

It started with an interview on KFI-640 am Los Angeles.

Bill Handle was interviewing the owner of a wedding dress shop called Curvaceous Couture, a "unique bridal salon where curvy brides experience the dream of finding the perfect wedding dress."

As I listened to them speaking, I thought, "Could they have chosen a harder name for their shop?" If someone wanted to find them, they had better be able to get close to the spellings of both words or they will be sent to a list of competitors. A quick search told me I was right. Including their own beta. curvaceouscoutureonline.com competing for the attention of their target audience.

That made me think—I wonder what other words people use in creating URLs that hurt them, just because their spelling is difficult. Our own Promotionally Minded is harder than it should be (that double L throws many people off) so there *has* to be a lot of them.

That thought let me to this test of the twenty-five most commonly misspelled words: http://www.businesswriting.com/tests/commonmisspelled.html.

I hit 74% but needed to guess on a bunch of them. We should not make it difficult for people to find us. Using dashes or underscores between words is *not* the answer, either. Promotionally_Minded.com would not make it a more user friendly web address because people do not think of adding dashes to your name.

And speaking of your name, if you have an odd spelling to your name and pop it into your URL, you may have difficulty, too. There is a financial planner in Los Angeles named Ric Edelman who has to tell people to go to "RicEdelman.com, or RiceDelman.com." The lack of a K on the end of his name has cost him hours of time in his radio ads, explaining it. Ric *was* brilliant enough to also purchase RickEdelman.com and have it redirect to his website.

So if you are putting together a website, here is a list of words, which are misspelled all the time, culled from various places—so re-check your spell check.

conscience

acceptable

definite

acknowledgment

advice

business

calendar

consensus

couture

develop

equipped

foreign

guarantee

identity

intelligent

lesson

neighbor

optimism

perceive

picture

privilege

reference

secretary

succeed

surprise

liaison

separate

withdrawal

committee

weird

warrantee

supersede

prerogative

occurrence

indispensable

existence

entrepreneur

recommend

accidentally

athlete

believe

certain

competition

commitment

curvaceous

dependent

excellent

forty*

happiness

immediately

invitation

license

occasion

original

permanent

practical

professional

restaurant

speech

successful

temporary

equipment

lightning

achieve

definitely

camouflage

publicly

separate

perseverance

liaison

inadvertent

connoisseur

mathematics

accommodate

argument

benefit

cemetery

convenience

deductible

desperate

embarrass

exercise

friend

harass

independent

knowledge

medicine

official

parallel

personally

prefer

psychology

rhythm

safety

village

unusual

gauge**

minuscule

welcome

surprise

existence

withhold

proceed

alchemist

judgment

foreword (as in a book)

Having multiple forms of the URL pointing to your primary site, is an inexpensive insurance policy—about $15 a year—to not lose someone who goes to the wrong site.

I am adding the word *alchemist* as a tip of the cap to my friend Cat Slater, the FashionAlchemist.com. Gee, Cat, couldn't you come up with a better word from this century?

How you *use* these words is yet another matter. For example: *breathe* and breath are both English words but are too often used interchangeably. Breathe (verb) refers to the act of inhaling and exhaling. Breath (noun) refers to the air coming in and out of the lungs.

For a discussion of those terms and the "their, there, they're, there're" and "to, two, and too" conundrums, check back in my next book!

I am prepared to win the next spelling bee.
○ YES   ○ NO

*If you are using the spelling of a number in your URL, you should also look for and purchase the Roman numeral as well, for example: Tools2Connect.com and ToolsTo-Connect.com, and for those who are very literal, ToolsTwoConnect.com.

** I cannot tell you how much I hate this word. I misspell it constantly.

35

Thirteen of the Top Ways to Get People to Come to Your First-Time Trade Show

So we were opening a division of our business in Arizona. And while we were getting established, there was a *cheap* opportunity to exhibit at a trade show. Here's the thing: For all I talk about trade shows, you would think that *cheap* would not be the reason we would exhibit there. But we did and there it is. The demographics of the people walking by our booth were going to be, by my estimation, less than 10% of our potential market. We wanted business owners and this was a B-to-C (business exhibiting to consumer) show. We wanted a thirty-five to fifty-five age group and the average here was sixty-plus. The only demographic in our favor was that most of the attendees lived within a prime distance for us. Going in, we knew this was a long weekend in the making. But we didn't know it was going to be *that* long.

This trade show was produced by a travel program for a local radio station that was doing the show for the first time, and they did it in a location that they were not familiar with. So for that station, here are a few tips.

1. Check out your competition. In this case, AAA was putting on a travel show on the same day. It was not their first time. They do this show every year at about the same time. It might have been a good thing to check their dates.

2. Check out what other events are going on at the same venue. In addition to this trade show, there was another, huge event going on right outside the door of this event.

3. One does not charge admission when your older, established competitor is free.

4. Don't charge for parking when your older, established competitor is free.

5. When you are a radio station putting on the event, it would probably be a great idea if you were to promote it on the station — in other

words generate buzz about the trade show internally. If I seem a little pissed here, it's because this was the most zero cost advertising they could have and they didn't do it.

6. Use a passport system to make sure people go to most of the booths. Offer prizes for the people who make the rounds of all the booths.

7. Signs. Have them. Everywhere. Big enough to see. This show did not have any signs on the main road leading to the venue. The signage outside the venue was nonexistent, which meant you would not know it if you had arrived there.

8. Visit the location for the event prior to move-in day. The person running the event for the station had never been to the venue. They knew the layout, but had no clue how to make the most of the building.

9. Include social sharing buttons on all promotions. This station did not mention the event on their social media pages.

10. Create a hash tag that will be used to market the event. Only use one. Give people a reason to use it—award prizes randomly for usage.

11. Create a targeted offer for the trade show. Come to this event and win prizes!

12. Promote with creativity. You have a trade show based on travel? Promote the idea of getting out of town by shopping in your home city.

13. Share the (F******) list. If you underperformed and got less than thousand people through the doors when you told your booth holders that there would be five to ten times that many, at least share the list of everyone who did come.

We always do research into who will attend a trade show prior to agreeing to take a booth.
◯ YES   ◯ NO

36

Choosing Your Retail Locations

I was on my way to an appointment on Ventura Boulevard in Los Angeles and while stopped at a light, I noticed a small retail space for rent. It was probably about twenty-five or thirty feet wide and had frontage on one of the most traveled roads in the city. But right in front was an equally wide red curb. That means that there is zero chance of having a client easily park and head right in. When going to your store, they are going to be met with the distraction and frustration of no parking.

In the Feng Shui world, that immediate barrier won't be acceptable. So when looking for a location, here is a checklist of things to be on the lookout for:

1. Parking. Plenty of *free* parking. I have a friend, Rickey Gelb, who owns several properties in the San Fernando Valley. He does not charge for parking in any of his buildings because, "It's hard enough for my tenants to make a living, why make it harder with them having to deal with parking. I would rather give them a reason to stay loyal to our buildings and company by helping them." While we are discussing it, how does that parking lot look? The client experience begins when they get to your parking lot. Is it paved or will they need to get new shocks in their car after visiting you?

2. Find a landlord like Rickey. Look, I know that men like Rickey Gelb are not that common. But if you are looking to move into a building, ask about the management. See if there are any patterns to their behavior with tenants. Too many red flags: *move on.* Like they say in relationships, do not look for someone you can fix. By the way, Rickey's number is 818-377-2277.

3. Obviously location is important. Are you asking your clients to travel a great distance? Sometimes you have to. With our Sedona Marketing Retreats business, we are asking people to fly or drive quite a distance (ninety minutes from Phoenix, three hours from Las Vegas, seven hours from Los Angeles, and fifteen hours from Dallas). The

tradeoff is a magical red rock setting. That is the exception.

If you are making your clients travel more than the average commute in your city for a product or service they can get much closer to home, then you better be the best of the best.

4. Check crime rates. Higher crime = lower rent in more ways than the check you will be writing each month.

5. Is the landlord willing to make improvements in the property? Ask for it all now because once you are moved in, you have lost all your leverage.

6. This may be silly, but where and when does the sun hit your windows? Are there times of the year this will be a pesky situation? In our Sedona Marketing Retreats office, there is an hour right after the sun comes up when we need to use a window treatment or we can't see the computer screen. The cat loves it though.

7. Look around before you decide. Use a map to decide where you are willing to put your business. How many competitors are in the area? How many complementary businesses (selling a different product to the same target market) are close by?

8. Time and pressure. How long before you open? Wow . . . it's getting late. Better hope you don't get pressured into picking the wrong place just because you need a place to unpack! Time is not your friend if you don't have the right place in plenty of time. Don't take space because you are under pressure—just postpone or work faster!

9. One thing you may not be able to control is who you share the building with. Heck, you could have new tenants move in *after* you. Check with the company that runs the building to see how long the other offices are leased because the companies that surround your company could affect how your customers perceive your business.

10. Signs are important. Negotiate for the largest, easiest to see sign you can. Does the building back up to a major highway? Get a sign that can be seen easily! You want to tell clients who are visiting to "just look for our sign on the building."

○ YES ○ NO

37

That's a Hard Act to Follow— Cliche in Marketing

It happens every month. Like clockwork. I can set my watch by it. We will be going around the room, doing self-introductions at some chamber or other meeting and right after someone says something remarkably pithy, which exudes laughter from the room, the next person will say, "That's a hard act to follow."

No. It is not.

Don't admit that you are not as talented. This morning, I *was* about to stand up to do a thirty-second intro, and the man in front of me sang his. And it was about animals. Abandoned animals.

As Homer Simpson would say, "*Doh!*"

It went through my head, damn it sucks to follow this guy, but I was not going to *say* that he was a hard act to follow. That is just trite. Instead, the woman introducing me said it. I just recognized it.

"There is a yellow elephant in the room," I began. "We are all fighting to get our marketing messages heard. And to do that you need to capture your target market's attention with a message that is not necessarily what they expect to hear or see. My name is Hank Yuloff. My wife, Sharyn, and I own Sedona Marketing—and that is what we specialize in doing: Getting your message in front of the right eyeballs to increase your sales."

Acknowledge it. Appreciate it. Use it to your advantage.

But that wasn't what this chapter was about. It is about how clichés trap us. They are our Achilles' heel. Using them takes away from our creativity in writing and does not allow our personality to be given the recognition it deserves (I almost wrote that it does not allow it to shine through). Worst of all, most of them refer to subjects which are terribly outdated and they make your communications look lazy. It is as if you could not come up with anything better to say, so you filled your document with jargon.

Here are a few that are very much overused. In other words, you should avoid them like the plague (I couldn't resist):

Out-of-the-Box.
Actions speak louder than words.

When push comes to shove.
All bets are off.
Red carpet treatment.
Selling like hotcakes.
Don't cry over spilt milk.
When it rains, it pours.
Every cloud has a silver lining.
Dressed to kill.
Throw in the towel.
It remains to be seen.
You could have knocked me over with a feather.
Raise the bar.
Right up your alley.
By the skin of your teeth.
Money does not grow on trees.
Win/win.
Failure is not an option.
Paradigm Shift.
Just be yourself.
Have a nice day.
What goes around, comes around.

And in the technical world, we are not immune to this slovenly communication, either:

LOL (laugh out loud)
ROFLMAO (rolling on floor laughing my ass off)
TTYL (talk to you later)
DDAS (don't do anything stupid)
DKDC (don't know, don't care)
GR8 (great)
FYI (for your information)

And one more, which I hope you did not do prior to picking up this book: Don't judge a book by its cover.

Are there some that bother you? Send me an email—I'm all ears!

Our marketing is so great, it's the best thing since sliced bread.
◯ YES ◯ NO

38

Santa's Elves—What the Heck Do They Do the Other Eleven Months of the Year?

I would like to share a holiday story with you that has the benefits of blogging as its marketing message. In order for this story to be most effective, though, you have to say out loud, "Hank, I believe in Santa Claus." Go ahead. I'll wait.

Ok, now to the story.

Many years ago, my good friend Santa Claus came to me and said, "Hank, you have been an exceptionally good boy—always on the Nice List (™ pending). For that reason, I want to hire you to solve a challenging situation I have been having for many years."

Intrigued, I sat down with the Jolly Old Elf and within an hour, we hit upon the solution to what had been vexing him. It seems that over the centuries, Santa's elves had gotten *very* good at their job of making toys. Couple that with the improvement in technology, and they were able to get all their work done in the two weeks prior to Santa's All Night Ride (as they call Christmas Eve at the North Pole—who knew?). As he was paying them for the entire year, Santa wanted to find a way to get a better return on his investment.

We brought Santa into the war room at Sedona Marketing Retreats and warmed up the magic white boards. As we worked on his demographics and marketing targets, one of Santa's very helpful partners kept popping up: Google.

We made a couple of phone calls and worked out an incredible marketing joint venture. Google had an issue that Santa could solve and within minutes, the deal was done.

Google's issue? They have thousands of searches to solve every second. And as good as their computers are, Santa's elves are *faster*!

So now, though you may not realize it, quite often when you type in a Google search, it is a group of Santa's elves who have a quick meeting to decide which websites have been naughty and which have been nice. So how, you may ask, do the Elves decide if a site is naughty or nice?"

That is the point of this blog! You see, one of the deal points that Google and Santa made prior to using the elves, was how would the toy-makers determine which websites would pop up on top. Google has a rule (and please note, this may change in future holiday seasons) that if a website is considered *relevant* then it shows up higher. Relevance is determined, among other things, by how often the website changes and is updated.

The logic goes like this: The more a company uses its website as a tool to interact with its clients, the more relevant their site. We have all seen websites that *don't* do this. They were built two, three, four, or more years ago and never change. They are rather like putting a picture of your business card online in case someone needs your phone number.

But, if a company is constantly sharing information with its clients on the website, then it is more relevant. One of the easiest ways for you to do this is by updating your blog page on a regular basis. We don't normally talk about our clients in public, but we have shared this story as a way to keep in your mind the benefits of blogging. Just remember: Santa knows when you are naughty and when you are nice, and blogging keeps you from getting a lump of coal in your stocking.

We are blogging our tails off so that the elves love us.
◯ YES   ◯ NO

39

Here Are Some Tips to Build a Website and Your Social Media Presence

A lot of our clients come to us with first-time websites built on non-growth platforms and we need to redo a lot of their work, which costs their time (at however they value it per hour), or whatever they paid for an inexperienced developer to build it, and it slows us down in preparing their marketing plan. These comments should be useful to you whether you are thinking of building your own website and social media pages, or having it outsourced by a professional, of which we can recommend several very good ones.

1. **Choose you website platform wisely.** There will come a time when you want to integrate different software with your website to automate your marketing, and you must know this: Not all software can be integrated with all platforms. Tumblr, Wix, Squarespace, etc., are very simple tools you can master with very little effort and time in order to build a beautiful website, but it will cost you scalability once you start to get traction. Use WordPress.

2. **Create a Fanpage and a Twitter account with your brand name.** You might not be getting traffic from social media right now, but you will want to once you're growing. Create a Facebook Fanpage and a Twitter account now, if only to reserve your desired username. Of course, if you can do it with Instagram, Pinterest, LinkedIn, StumbleUpon, and others, it is a great idea, too.

3. **Connect your site with Google Analytics.** There's no need for you to understand Analytics on day one, but sooner than later you (or your growth hacker) will need some insights about your visitor's behavior. If you wait until you need that data, you will start collecting data at that point, in other words, all previous data won't be accessible.

4. **Connect your site with Google Webmaster Tools.** Same as Analytics, but for SEO. You might or might not be working proactively

on improving your SEO when you're launching, but it will be important in the near future. Do yourself a favor and start collecting data from the first day.

5. **Install Facebook's and Adwords's retargeting pixel.** This is one of the coolest things ever to someone who thinks advertising done right is incredible. You have seen how they work. Let's say you go to Amazon and look up a Canon camera. You spend ten minutes or so reading about the various models in preparation of purchasing. Then you leave the website, but all of a sudden on Facebook and most everywhere else you turn, ads for Canon cameras pop up on the side of your screen. It's not as *if* the ads are following you, they *are* following you around the internet. When you install a retargeting pixel, a list with all your visitors begins to be gathered so that you can target them later with ads. The problem is that all the traffic that was previous to the installation is excluded from that list, so do it now, regardless of whether or not you want to use retargeting right now.

All of this internet stuff can become overwhelming, but our company has a handle on it.

◯ YES   ◯ NO, we really need some help.

40

I Blogged—What Else Can I Do with It? The Art of Repurposing

The previous chapter comes from a story I have been telling for a while. I needed to tell a story in my marketing boot camps and seminars that graphically explained one of the reasons for people to blog—that their websites needed to be relevant by changing often.

So how was I going to visually explain how Google and other search engines worked? Santa and his elves! By saying that it was the elves that made the decisions, I am giving the search engines a face.

Since it was a good story, I figured out other ways to use it. It's called repurposing, the reuse of content you created once for several other purposes. Remember in grade school when using the same report for two purposes was frowned upon? Well, not when you are a grown up, it is appreciated.

The Santa and the elves story has been used a few ways so far. I tell it live. I used it to create a blog. I made a short video telling the story. Two chapters in this book. And I will also continue to use it in other ways. It is called repurposing. In one sentence, repurposing is putting content and information you have created once, to use in several ways. The reason we repurpose information is that with so many outlets to gather information, it is *highly* probable that your audience would not see your information if you only presented it once.

That's where your weekly, monthly (or how often you decide) e-newsletter or printed newsletter comes in. It's where your blog, which is being shared to your social media comes in. And then it gets shared in your book. And on your radio show. And when you present to live audiences.

So, once they opt-in to your information on your website, they start getting your newsletter, which has:

- The most recent blog post with an invitation to comment, plus a link to the post on your website.
- Two testimonials from clients, the written version plus the link to the video.
- Chapters from your books.
- Information about upcoming sales, deadlines, new products, new

resources, anything that is new or is vital for them to have.

- Cool ideas. For example, our company can provide fun ways to say happy birthday to a client with links to our SendOutCards account (www.CardsByHank.com), or ways to exhibit at a trade show, or ways to show appreciation.
- An event list (upcoming retreats, radio show, blab broadcasts, conferences—with links).
- How to become an affiliate plus a link.
- This month's most interesting social media posts. For me it could be the most fun Ok, Late Night Facebooker's answers. Ok, Late Night Facebookers is a fun question of the night that I have been posting since 2010.
- Brilliant-client-idea-of-the-month—who's doing what, creatively to promote their company using stuff we provide, or not, if it's a great idea, let's share it.
- Whatever else you want to share.

Most of the items on that list can be repurposed from other activities you're *already* doing. I like to think of it as a print (albeit digitally-printed) version of my radio show. The content could even be the same!

I discussed newsletters in *The Marketing Checklist*. They are a great idea. It's smart to remember that people learn differently. A vast majority of our society learns *visually*. Reading and looking at pictures, in most cases. Some don't have the flexibility to go to your live events. Some don't have time to listen to a live show or scan through an audio recording for the good stuff, but perhaps they *do* have time to look at an e-newsletter on their iPhone while sitting in the library.

We are repurposing our blogs even more so that the elves love us.
◯ YES ◯ NO

41

There's No Need to Advertise When You Create a Wookie

The best kind of business is one where you have a very loyal following, willing to buy your product or service over and over, potentially caused by a limited amount of new product, which allows for price inelasticity, a limited amount of competition, and no need to advertise.

The Model T Ford was such a product. Until all those other cars made on production lines lowered prices for other vehicles, Henry Ford created a car that was priced so that his employees could actually buy one. Toyota had one for a while, in the Prius.

Another product is Disneyland. Admittedly, they have less elasticity and they are controlling attendance by raising their prices. But no other amusement parks have the same kind of atmosphere and, of course, a big 'ol mouse in red pants, which keeps their target audience coming back for more.

Apple has one of these products, its iPhone. Loyal devotees will wait in line for *days* for a new edition, pumping a billion dollars into the computer company.

The best of these products don't have the kind of competition that should cause them to advertise very often, and some of these products should do not need anything more than a few dozen press releases to fill the coffers of the manufacturing company.

For a short period of time, Beanie Babies were this way. There are not many of these products or companies around, but one of them is launching a new product that is going to bring in $1billion by the end of the year: It is the seventh and latest Star Wars movie—*Star Wars the Force Awakens*, and is about as sure a money-printing machine as any product ever produced.

There has not been a new *Star Wars* movie for either seven years (*Star Wars: The Clone Wars*) or ten years (*Episode III: Revenge of the Sith*) depending on which fan you listen to — and I have witnessed social media arguments debating this and many other *Star Wars* facts — and the consumers of this product cannot open their wallets fast enough.

I have heard people want to see the movie several times over opening weekend and I have spoken to a few friends who feel like they *have* to see it so they keep up with what everyone else is going to be talking about at work.

That second fact reminded me of why I went to see *Titanic* (the boat sinks, by the way).

What *Star Wars* does is get all of us to ask ourselves how much we would love to create a product that our customers are such raving fans that they cannot get enough of us. If the answer is *yes*, then keep Darth Vader, Luke, Leia, Han, and Jabba in your mind when you are writing that book, putting together that marketing plan, designing your store, or creating your list of services.

I expect that the next two questions are *why*? And *how*? Why are the *Star Wars* movies such a magnet for our credit cards and how can you create a product that does the same thing. I wish I could give you a definite answer, but this quote from Peter Drucker will have to do: "The aim of marketing is to know and understand the customer so well that product or service fits him and sells itself."

Oh, and for those Star Trekkies who are dying to ask me if their franchise reaches the same level of George Lucas' creations, my answer is this: Only if Kirk and Spock are in it.

There, *that* ought to get the comments going.

The Force is with our marketing.
○ YES   ○ NO, we need a Jedi to help us.

42

Keeping Our Head in the Marketing Game

Not everything you do to market your business has to be a major undertaking. I came up with an idea that won't make us a lot of money, but it certainly makes people think about us.

I have talked about using logo'd wearables to promote your company before. In a marketing book, I know it seems a bit self-serving for the owner of a promotional products company to say you should use them, but hang with me for a bit.

When it comes to giving out t-shirts with your logo, I shared earlier that I am of the opinion that unless you have a well-known name, a brand that people truly relate to, that they are not going to wear it often. But here is something you can do to get someone to wear your name.

Sometimes it is not what it *is*, but it is what it *says*. I have been able to stand up in front of an audience and make the promise that "Even the most shy person in the audience can have people walk up to them and ask what they do." When that most reticent person is located, I hand them a t-shirt that says "*My Clients All Want to Hug Me*" emblazoned across the front. It makes an instant connection with all who see it, and our logo goes along for the ride at the bottom of the shirt (and off to the side). In this case, my promotional product's *imprint* was what made the product memorable and useful.

We always look for ways to keep our head in the marketing game.
◯ YES ◯ NO

43

The Project Checklist—Preparing for the Job

We work with a lot of service businesses: web and home designers, meeting planners, building trades, coaches, and attorneys. We talk a lot about how they put together budgets for their client's projects. For them, and you, it is important to stay within those budgets in order to make a profit. No use working for nothing, right? If you stay within those budgets, and not let them creep out of the parameters, you will be profitable.

Here are some tips to help you avoid going over budget:

1. Review the factors that go in to your estimates prior to beginning the proposal. Include all deliverables—the resources, services, and materials you will provide; the resources, services, and materials your client will provide; an in-hands or completion date; prices; contingencies, which could affect that price; and terms of payment. Know that your factors will change from time to time.

2. Be sure to involve all the stakeholders up front. This includes sales people and support team so that everyone will be on that proverbial "same page."

3. We have talked about creating your marketing schedule before. Here, specify the things that need to be done and their due dates. It's best to get buy in from the client and make sure that they are able to get every question answered.

4. Make sure the client knows what is *not* included in the project so that these little add-ons do not take apart your profit. Use your best judgement on the client as to whether or not a fee will be charged for this unplanned work.

5. Decide on who will be on the project team from your company and from the client's company. Determine who is authorized to sign off on approvals and changes in the original contract.

94

6. Set up approval points and times for when the project is moving along. This way you can determine if you are on budget and it reminds the client what information they need to provide your team.

7. If you are *not* on track, that is the time to correct it. This is why we have gotten top decision makers involved early, because they are the ones who will, Murphy's Law kicking in, want to make the most changes at the most expensive time. If you have gotten them involved early, you can then point out the costs (time and money) in making their proposed changes, and many times they will decided that the change is not all that important.

We have a bid or proposal checklist.
◯ YES   ◯ NO

44

A Lesson in Camera-Ready Artwork

When we are printing promotional products on plastic, or brochures and flyers on paper the saying I have always used with clients regarding artwork is that "As good as you give me is as good as you get." I want to stress to business owners that in preparing to print their collateral materials, we need to make them look great on the screen in order for them to look great in real life, but what looks good on a computer screen does not necessarily look good when it is *off* screen.

It is not a difficult concept to explain, but most people in our industry do not know *how* to explain the concept of printable artwork. I thought I would share some thoughts on it here.

A bit of history first, and then on to the good news. Our industry spent a century teaching our clients the definition of camera-ready artwork. As the term denotes, at one time a camera was used to prepare artwork for printing. Having the part of your artwork that was going to print in black on a bright white background was the best. We would use a mathematical formula to make sure our type came out of the linotype machine at the proper size, then place it under a camera to prepare the printing plates.

As the printing process has evolved, this has changed dramatically. We no longer use cameras, and are able to go directly from the computer screen to creating plates for paper printing, and screens for silk screening.

The most important thing to remember is to begin with the end in mind. What material are you printing on? A computer screen can make your artwork one way, but when it comes to the printing process, the laws of physics begin to apply. Something that looks good on screen will probably look good on a high gloss paper which has very few pores for the ink to sink into. A rougher paper—like the paper in most printers—will absorb more ink and the image can spread. Picture pouring a bottle of Pepto Bismol onto a paper towel. You may only pour onto a one-inch square, but it expands to cover a larger area. On a micro scale, ink and paper does the same thing. On plastic, it does the opposite. Plastic has tiny pores, so ink will spread over a larger area and fill in if you do not have properly prepared your artwork. A half-tone image is a screen that is used on a half-tone block and separates the image into different size dots. Here is an example of what I mean:

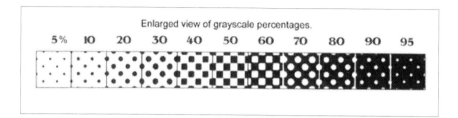

Enlarged view of grayscale percentages.

5% 10 20 30 40 50 60 70 80 90 95

This is why you can have so many different shades of gray.

Here are a few tips to make sure you are happier with your artwork:

1. If you can, use solid tone ink. Solid tone has no pixilation. When you look very closely at a photograph, you will see that it is comprised of millions of little dots, which, when viewed from a distance, seem to be a rainbow of slightly different colors. We call this a half-tone (half the image is ink, the other half is paper showing through). Solid tones are ink sitting on top of the material without letting any of the material (paper, plastic, cloth) show through. Generally a much brighter result.

2. If you are going to use half-tones, make sure that the number of those dots is proper for the material you are going to print on. The printing term is dots per inch. On a computer screen, 72 dpi (dots per inch) works great. On high gloss paper, that number goes up into the hundreds. 300 dpi is a standard for much better printing. For plastic, you cannot expect to use a screen because the ink dots will merge. Remember the physics.

3. When someone asks for your artwork or your logo, don't "right click, save" from your website. That is going to be 72 dpi or less and will cause delays in your printing because the printer is going to have to adjust (another word for re-create and charge you for it) your artwork.

4. Don't do this yourself. If you are printing, find a graphic artist with experience in printing. In the computer age, we are seeing artists

who can do magnificent things on a computer screen, but have no idea how to prepare their artwork for printing.

5. Learn a couple of terms. A jpg is a photo. It is made up of pixels. If you are printing your artwork and it includes photos or if your solid tone artwork has been saved as a jpg by your inexperienced graphic artist, you will be disappointed. If you are printing something, it is generally better to use the electronic equivalent of camera-ready artwork. This is called *vector* art. The term comes from the world of mathematics where, as the artwork gets larger, it remains the same. Want to see an example? Take a photograph and make it a *lot* larger than its 100% size. You will start to see it get fuzzy. The pixels are getting further and further apart and the quality drops dramatically.

6. Here is the best news—understand that the printing industry is changing drastically. Because photo copiers have improved so much, we are starting to see full color digital printing create photographic quality products. We are seeing improved printing processes come into the promotional products world, which is making our products more effective. The bad news? You still need a graphic artist to make sure the artwork is created correctly in the first place.

7. Don't settle. Saying "I just needed something to . . ." is not going to make you look as professional as you deserve to be seen.

Make sure you get all your artwork done properly.

We have our logo in all the different formats, ready to be easily shared with a vendor.
○ YES   ○ NO

45

Forty-nine of My Favorite Marketing Quotes

Hey, you have been doing some great work so far, so let's take a quick break and feed our minds some positivity and inspiration.

> *"The aim of marketing is to know and understand the customer so well, the product or service sells itself."*
> Peter Drucker

One of my absolute favorite quotes. Asking our clients why they buy from us can be scarier than asking why they *didn't* buy from us.

> *"Marketing without data is like driving with your eyes closed."*
> Dan Zarrella

> *"Measuring engagement and engaging consumers are two sides of the same coin."*
> David Penn

Without showing clients we care, and getting them involved in what we do, we do not get repeat business. If they like us, how much to they like us?

> *"Quality is doing it right when no one is looking."*
> *"You can't build a reputation on what you are going to do."*
> *"A business that makes nothing but money is a poor business."*
> Henry Ford

These quotes remind me that each time I go on to the commerce playing field to help a client, it is their success that we seek. That is what, in the end, makes me smile and gives me the inspiration to do even better for the next client.

> *"Research is formalized curiosity. It is poking and prying with a purpose."*
> Zora Neale Hurston

Feasibility studies? Competitive assessments? Customer surveys? Each are built on the premises of the unknown. Market research is a perfect starting point.

"Research is about engaging in a conversation with a brand."
Matthew Rhodes

"Without data you're just another person with an opinion."
W. Edwards Deming

We hear so often that you have to trust your gut. I think it is easier to trust that trust if you have more than a hunch to go on.

"Your most unhappy customers are your greatest source of learning."
Steve Jobs

When I speak to groups, I love getting high numbers on the evaluation forms. But I learn more from the comments and the less than perfect scores. In fact, the only refund check I ever wrote (out of hundreds of attendees) for the 5 Star Guarantee we offer at Promotionally Minded Marketing Days taught me a bunch that I could improve on.

"The older I get, the less I listen to what people say
and the more I look at what they do."
Andrew Carnegie

"People often say that motivation doesn't last. Well, neither does bathing—that's
why we recommend it daily."
Zig Ziglar

We need constant reminders of the right way, and the consistent way of getting our job done. It's one reason I have this chapter in here—to give us all some "written energy" to keep moving.

"Don't use big words. They mean so little."
Oscar Wilde

We talked about the importance of using surveys to gather important information about our customers and target audiences. The objective of writing a survey is to relate to the respondent, engage them, and fish out information. This is a reminder that the objective of writing a survey is not to have the survey taker finish and say "there were words on that paper that I didn't know existed. Wow, that survey writer is certainly astute."

"Management is doing things right; leadership is doing the right things."
Peter Drucker

"Doing a common thing uncommonly well brings success."
Henry John Heinz

*"When you innovate, you've got to be prepared
for everyone telling you you're nuts."*
Larry Ellison

These next twelve quotes were found on Larry Broughton's leadership website—Yoogozi.com. You should bookmark that site!

"Smooth seas never made a skillful sailor."

"Your word: Live up to it, or own up to it."

"Seek progress, not perfection."

*"Great leaders acknowledge that they must be of service to others
in order to achieve greatness."*

"If we don't take a chance, we don't stand a chance."

"A wise person knows that there is something to be learned from everyone."

*"We need to take a great interest in the future
because we'll spend the rest of our life there."*

"Efficiency is intelligent laziness."

"Remember, everybody roots for David, nobody roots for Goliath."

"Don't assume the competition knows your weaknesses."

"If you're going to rise, you might as well shine."

*"If you think you are too small to be effective,
you have never been in the dark with a mosquito."*

"When you feel like quitting, think about why you started."

"Never apologize for having high standards. People who really want to be in your life will rise up to meet them."

*"Most marketers create 'good enough' and then quit.
Greatest beats 'good enough' every time."*
Seth Godin

"Traditional marketing talks at people. Content marketing talks with them."
Doug Kessler

*"Culture is to employees as product is to consumers.
And culture is rooted in collaboration and trust."*

"Stealth mode is for fighter jets, not startups."

"Make the customer the hero of your story."
Ann Handley

*"Either write something worth reading about
or do something worth writing about."*
Benjamin Franklin

*"If you want to understand how a lion hunts, don't go to the zoo.
Go to the jungle."*
Jim Stengel

"If everyone is thinking alike, then somebody isn't thinking."
General George Patton

"The best marketing doesn't feel like marketing."
Tom Fishburne

"Content isn't king. It's the kingdom."
Lee Odden

*"Traditional marketing and advertising is telling the world you're a rock star.
Content Marketing is showing the world that you are one."*
Robert Rose

"Don't find customers for your products, find products for your customers."
Seth Godin

"Whether you think you can, or think you can't, you're right."

"If plan "A" fails, remember you have twenty-five letters left."
Chris Guillebeau

And finally . . . five important ones for me.

"Marketing is a science of choice. It's letting people pre-disposed to buying your product or service know that you are there for them."
Hank Yuloff

"Tell a story. We are hard-wired to accept stories."

"Always start with the end in mind."

"My greatest strength as a consultant is to be ignorant and ask a few questions."
Peter Drucker

This has always reminded me that going in to a situation where we are creating a marketing plan or teaching a marketing boot camp intensive, we may be awesome at what we do, but we cannot have all the answers prior to investigating the client's needs.

"The mountains ahead are easier to climb when we take a moment to remember the trail that led us there."
Hank Yuloff

I am ready and motivated to take the next steps in our marketing.
◯ YES   ◯ NO

Want to Know How You Can Score from Non-Profits?

I use this phrase all the time when I speak in public. Quite often, I get a bit of a shocked look on a few faces. Score from a non-profit? But they are doing good deeds, why should we be benefiting from them?

I am not saying to benefit at the expense of non-profits. I am saying to use your talents to support them and build your person-to-person network while you do it. You have heard the simple sales rule, right? "People like to do business with people they like."

When you work on a non-profit with other people, you have something in common and that helps your cause.

So volunteer for a cause that means something to you. At their events, work the registration table so you get to meet everyone. Donate items to their silent auction.

You can also give away your service. From time to time, I will stand up at one of the networking meetings I attend and say that I will donate my time to a grass-roots non-profit that needs marketing assistance. There are certain requirements (board size, have to be currently operating—not just an idea, certain systems in place) but I am quite willing to give back. I am here to tell you that when you give away, you do get back.

We appreciate non-profits and they are part of our marketing strategy.
◯ YES ◯ NO

Non-Profits Need to Change Their Attitude

Non-profits are always busy building their business by helping to improve their client's lives and helping their community succeed, without much back up. How about focusing on your organization's success for a while?

In our family, there was a strong commitment to assist non-profits in accomplishing their mission. One of my early television memories is our family watching the yearly KCET (Los Angeles, channel 28) pledge drive and auction each year and debating on which items to bid on. It was more than just making a donation, it was supporting an organization that was important to us.

That early introduction to non-profits stuck. When it comes to clients for our marketing-plan and promotional-product companies, trade unions, school organizations, associations, youth groups, and business and religious organizations have all found their way through our doors, and continue to be our clients. Sharyn has her master in business administration focusing on non-profits and between the two of us we have served on the boards of seven of them. Our promotional product company, Promotionally Minded, has always had a policy that 10% of our time, effort, and revenue goes toward servicing non-profits (the actual number has worked out to be 12%).

Our expert familiarity and appreciation for the work that non-profits do makes this one of the most exciting client industries for us to work with.

When it comes to marketing, we feel that the term non-profit is best remembered to be a tax-status and creating a profitable situation for the organization is vitally important.

Here are a few points for your non-profit checklist:

1. Your board of directors must be large enough. A board of five, six, or even nine is not enough because of the specific talents you need.

2. The makeup of your board is important. You need to have financial people, (accountants, bankers, financial planners). You need legal people (contracts, business, and depending on the non-profit you should look at other topics). You need someone who can help you

with your marketing. You need people who are affected by your mission so they can sell your message. You need local political leaders or those who are connected to them.

3. You need to work on your message and it has to be more than "we serve the X community." Why give to your non-profit? Why not give to another organization who does the same thing? Or not give at all.

4. Are there other non-profits in your area that cover the same community? Most times when I ask a non-profit this question, I get the "Yeah, but . . . ," answer and then I hear a long explanation as to why they are different and better. Here is my suggestion: Develop a strong relationship and work together. Remember, the idea is to serve the community, not necessarily who gets it done.

5. Non-profits have always had to have a "do more with less" attitude. It's okay to have that feeling, but why not have an attitude of prosperity instead of poverty?

6. For a list of fundraising ideas, check out my book, *The Marketing Checklist: 80 Simple Ways to Master Your Marketing.*

**Now, we *really* appreciate non-profits
and they are part of our marketing strategy.**
◯ YES ◯ NO

48

Event Checklist

From time to time, you are going to take part in an event for a group or hold one for own company. Here is a checklist of things to have covered.

1. Designate the event planner or coordinator.

2. Establish your budget. Everything will be determined by this.

3. Set event date and time. Establish a bad-weather date, if necessary.

4. Gain sponsorships. What do the sponsors get for their dollars?

5. Delegate responsibilities:
   - a. Designate a contact for RSVPs
   - b. Prepare guest list
   - c. Choose parking assistants
   - d. Choose greeters / information table / check in
   - e. Choose emcee / speakers
   - f. Who will be in charge of VIP
   - g. Who is in charge of clean up

6. Plan activates.

7. Get your local chamber of commerce involved.

8. Select and contact event vendors:
   - a. Caterer
   - b. Photographer
   - c. Videographer
   - d. Florist
   - e. Entertainment / musicians
   - f. Rentals
   - g. Security
   - h. Decorations

9. Predetermine the event layout (where to place tables, chairs, stage, podium).
   - a. Determine the number of tables, chairs, trash cans needed.

and where they will be placed.

    b. Plan the setup of any A/V equipment and screen.

10. Prepare any materials needed for the event:
    a. Visuals
    b. Awards
    c. Checks
    d. Documents
    e. Gifts
    f.. Samples
    g. Locate company sign or banners
    h. Name tags
    i. Ribbon and scissors for grand openings

11. Design and send invitations:
    a. Deadline to get invitations to printers
    b. Time needed to prepare mailing list and labels
    c. Date to mail/ email / fax invitations

12. Set date to call or send reminders.

13. Prepare press releases to go out two to four weeks in advance

14. Identify dates to contact local media:
    a. Prepare list
    b. Notify media with invitations to attend

15. Post event tasks:
    a. Follow up with thank you notes to all of your speakers, sponsors and other VIPs who attended, as well as your staff.
    b. Share your photos and videos by posting them online, including them in your newsletter and all appropriate means of getting your news out.
    c. Send a post-event news release with photos of your event to your local media.

16. Wrap up evaluation—meet to determine how to improve the event.

We are prepared for our next event.
◯ YES ◯ NO

49

It's Time to Call for Action

This chapter is towards the end of the book because I want to give you a reminder and a call to action.

"Call to action?" some may say. "But Hank, I bought your book and now I have even *read* it. Isn't that enough?" You know my answer.

Let's start with one target. For this exercise, I want you to visualize one target market segment. Use these demographic traits to define that segment: age, sex, income, number of children, race or ethnicity, education, marital status, and location. Here is a checklist for what you should do now.

1. Develop the Unique Selling Proposition designed for this target market.

2. Pick the five things in this book, and in its companion book, *The Marketing Checklist: 80 Simple Ways to Master Your Marketing*, that you feel will be a combination of A) easy, and B) most effective for your business in reaching that one audience. Easy because I know that if it is too difficult, it will not get done. This is going to be a theme in a book I will write later that has to do with what physics teaches us about marketing. In this case, Newton's *First* Law of Motion: "When viewed in aninertial reference frame, an object either remains at rest or continues to move at a constant velocity, unless acted upon by an external force." That means we have to get you moving in *some* direction.

3. Don't wait too long to contact a lead. Every year, I attend a promotional product convention in August put on by an industry organization. And every year, in November or December or January, I get two to three calls from factories who say that they are following up on my stopping at their booth three to five months earlier. My ability to remember what I saw at one trade show booth out of four hundred after that period of time is minimal. How long should you wait? Don't. Call now.

4. And keep calling. Follow up is vital. Repetitive studies show that the sale is made on the tenth to twelfth contact. Yes, that sucks, but in this case, human nature brings us back to physics and Newton's *third* law: "When one body exerts a force on a second body, the second body simultaneously exerts a force equal in magnitude and opposite in direction on the first body." In other words, your clients are buying from somewhere that is not you, and you are trying to change their habits. So the more quickly you contact a lead, the more likely you get this process going and the faster you will make the sale.

5. Use various methods to contact them. We have talked about a bunch of different marketing tactics. Remembering that we are all different and that not all tactics work every time, you want to increase your odds.

6. Change the offer. Give those potential clients different specials on different services that you offer. One of my favorite things to do is send four offers: a $50 off first-promotional product order, $100 off the second order, some offer introducing our marketing services, and a copy of one of my books just for having me stop by to say hello. That is sort of my free-gift-with-order without them having to spend a dime.

7. Seek sales or marketing coaching to help you with the skills you want refined. There are some great coaches out there, make sure they have been in sales successfully for a long while.

8. Don't wait for me to have my book on physics and marketing published before you start. Go get them!

I did the exercise.
◯ YES   ◯ NO—I'll read this chapter again.

50

Bonus: Customers Are . . .

We have always run our small business with the understanding that some companies, when they get too large, tend to forget. We all exist to serve a customer. If we are not taking away our client's pain, they have no reason to give us a check. I wanted to share with you the description of what we feel about our clients.

Customers are the most important part of our business. They are the reason we have a job. Customers are not an interruption of our work, they are the purpose for our work. Customers do us a favor by giving us the opportunity to serve their needs.

They are not dependent on us, we are dependent on them. If we don't care for our customers, someone else will.

1. My customers are clients, employees, and co-workers.

2. I make customers' needs and objectives come first.

3. I make myself available and accessible to all.

4. I greet customers courteously, using my name.

5. I treat complaints and objections as opportunities.

6. I follow through by communicating and confirming.

7. I put myself in my customer's shoes.

8. I do so because I want to, not have to.

9. I never say "no," I seek solutions.

10. I listen, interpret, clarify, and pursue solutions.

11. I express appreciation.

12. The customer is my greatest priority!

We will save you money whenever possible. We will do our best to make your artwork perfect. We will bring you promotional product ideas that will market you well. We will give you distribution plans which make sense. Whenever there is a mistake or miscommunication, we believe that the customer is always right.

Listen to your customers and understand your demographics. Going out of your way to make one customer feel happy will result in good word-of-mouth that you could never buy.

That's our description. What is yours like?

We have a firm understanding of who our customer is and have shared that with everyone who works for us.
○ YES   ○ NO

Epilogue

Finally

Using this book and its predecessor — *The Marketing Checklist: 80 Simple Ways to Master Your Marketing* will show you lots of ways to chart out your marketing plans. A little research on either of our websites, OurMarketing-Guy.com or SedonaMarketingRetreats.com and you can get lots more help.

On that note, thank you for reading this book. I hope you have gotten a lot out of it. If you have some important marketing questions, head to our website, and submit it on our marketing questions page.

Life requires business.

Business requires marketing.

Marketing is education.

Education creates value.

Value is the only thing that sells.

Sales is service.

Service is a noble thing.

What pain do you remove from your customer? That is what they are paying you for.

About the Author

Hank Yuloff is a targeted marketing tactician with over thirty years experience keeping companies "top of mind" with their customers.

In high school, after winning a writing contest to attend a Beatrice Foods stockholders meeting as a field trip, Hank Yuloff was given a Cross pen and pencil set with the corporate logo as a remembrance. Years later that meeting continues to shape his career.

After graduating from San Diego State University with a degree in advertising and public Relations he began his career working for two newspapers and then became a President's Club member for both a direct mail company and a promotional products company (he was also one of their sales managers) before opening Promotionally Minded, in 1997. They specialize in targeted marketing plans, logo development, client retention and appreciation programs, and run a nationally recognized promotional products company (that pen and pencil set got the ball rolling). All of these brands have been combined into the Sedona Marketing moniker (SedonaMarketingRetreats.com).

He has many years of board of director experience for several non-profit organizations. Hank has received numerous awards for public service, including the Tami Ginsburg Celebration of Service award by the United Chambers of Commerce of Los Angeles. The award is given to the individual who, from amongst the twenty-three member chambers, has shown a continued involvement in many facets of the community as a volunteer.

He is the author of two previous books *49 Stupid Things People Do with Business Cards... and How to Fix Them* and *The Marketing Checklist: 80 Simple Ways to Master Your Marketing*, which became a New Arrivals Best Seller on Amazon.com. Hank and his wife of twenty-five years, Sharyn, host a weekly radio show with the same name (*The Marketing Checklist*). It can be found at TheMarketingChecklist.com.

They are very excited to have opened a new branch of their company called Sedona Marketing Retreats. That company creates two types of three and a half-day events. For partner-owned small businesses, they create custom marketing plans in a highly focused, one-on-one setting *and* they also host small group marketing boot camps in a mastermind setting for similar, major demographic entrepreneurs.

Several times a year, they speak to larger groups throughout the United States. Hank and Sharyn were very excited to have the opportunity to appear in an entrepreneurial mini-series with international training expert and best-selling author Brian Tracy called *Live Your List* in the fall of 2016.

And he still has that pen and pencil set!

Other Books by Hank Yuloff
49 Stupid Things People Do with Business Cards… And How to Fix Them
The Marketing Checklist: 80 Simple Ways to Master Your Marketing

Leave Me a Review!

If you enjoyed this book or found it useful, please don't keep me a secret. I'd appreciate it if you would take a moment to leave a review on Amazon. I'm always interested in learning what you like, think, and want. I read all the reviews personally.

Thank you for your support!

You can reach us at info@SedonaMarketing.com.